W9-AFR-448

Thanksgiving 1959

When One Corner of New York City Was Still Part
of Small-Town America, and High School Football
Was the Last Thing Guys Did for Love

JAY PRICE

A Mountain Lion Book

Mountain Lion Inc.
P.O. Box 799
Pennington, N.J. 08534

Library of Congress Control Number: 2009930615
ISBN: 978-0-9770039-3-8

Book design by Christopher Johnson
Manufacturing by RR Donnelley

First Edition: 2009

10 9 8 7 6 5 4 3 2 1

*To Sal Somma, whose players weren't the
only ones he inspired.*

To Pop, who passed along his love of the games.

*And Mud, who doesn't remember all she did for me ...
which is OK, because I do.*

Foreword

It's always more fun reading about one of the good guys, instead of some of those other guys we hear so much about these days.

That's what this book is.

I wasn't a football guy growing up, so I didn't get to know Sal Somma as a person until later on in life. I thought of him mostly as the guy who kicked the big "extra point."

When I did get to know him, he was everything I'd heard about: an honest, down to earth person who believed in doing what's right, the way my own dad brought my older brother and me up. In short, a very decent man who set a wonderful example for young people to follow.

This book reminds me of the way I always felt about the guy, and the way everybody felt about him, and the stories take me back to the place where I grew up.

~BOBBY THOMSON
New York Giants

1951 Shot Heard Round the World
in Giant-Dodger N.L. Playoff

Contents

Part
I

1
Three from '59

There was no missing them, the middle-aged men in their dark suits, and those just pushing middle age, sitting with the rest of the mourners in St. Clare's Church that frosty February morning in 1993.

These were Sal Somma's guys, the ones who were drawn to him as teenagers by whatever it was that made them think they wanted to play high school football ... because their friends were on the team, or it was what guys did in those days, going from baseball to football to basketball according to the season ... because it was the one place in the world where they felt like they were as good as everybody else, or like they belonged ... or they just wanted the chance to knock the snot out of somebody and not get in trouble for it ... and were changed forever by the experience, in ways they didn't fully understand when it was happening.

Now they'd come to say goodbye.

"A piece of America died yesterday," the story in the Staten Island Advance began.

"That's what Sal Somma was.

"He was the part that said in this country it was possible for anyone, no matter how poor, to make something of themselves with hard work and a little direction.

"And that there was a right way to do it."

And who better to pass along those lessons than a high school dropout and teenage runaway who wound up becoming a legendary teacher and coach, and a role model to generations of kids … many of them, like him, the children of immigrants … all because of football.

For them, it only made it more meaningful to remember that at the other end of an improbable life, Somma kicked the extra point that kept Vince Lombardi and Fordham's legendary "Seven Blocks of Granite" out of the Rose Bowl at a time when there were only two sports that mattered in America, and college football was one of them, even in New York City. Especially in New York, where all the big sportswriters lived and worked, and tens of thousands of New Yorkers who never set foot on a college campus filled Yankee Stadium or the Polo Grounds whenever Notre Dame came to town to play Army; or when the local schools, Fordham, NYU, and Columbia, played host to the best college teams in the country.

The men sitting in the polished pews at St. Clare's were teachers and firemen and politicians and stock brokers, with wives and kids and jobs to get back to, and mortgages to pay. One of Sal's guys piloted the plane that helped rescue Gemini 8 astronauts Neil Armstrong and Dave Scott after an emergency splashdown in the western Pacific, three years before Armstrong walked on the moon. Another played in the Super Bowl. A few were millionaires. A lot of them were the first in their families to go to college.

But in this setting, in the company of men they played and

fought and laughed and cried with, when they were all just boys — stripped naked five afternoons a week and again on Saturday, because on those days there was no place to hide who you were, and no way to fake it — they were transported back to a time when it didn't matter if they were rich or poor, or if their parents belonged to the Country Club or they just got off the boat from the Old Country.

A part of each of them was 17 again, sitting in some unheated locker room with the old fears rising in the pit of his stomach, listening to the whooping and hollering coming from down the hall, and hoping he'd find the calm, and the courage ... again ... to do whatever had to be done without screwing things up for everybody else, and that he wouldn't do anything to disappoint the man in the coat and tie and the gray fedora.

One time or another, if they're lucky, everybody who plays a team sport feels that sense of fraternity, and assumes it will last forever, and it hardly ever does. But the guys from New Dorp High School, where Somma worked for 29 years and won a bunch of New York City championships at a time when people still took notice of such things, and even the venerable *New York Times* chronicled the games, felt that bond more than most.

The gang from the 1959 team was especially close, vacationing and celebrating holidays together, and standing up at each other's weddings; still best friends, all those years later, so when they looked back they could see that was part of Somma's gift, too. Along with everything else, he'd given them each other.

Some of that was on Joe Avena's mind, that day in the church. Of all Somma's players, he might've felt the deepest sense of obligation. For somebody who had nothing as a child, Avena counted himself lucky. Lucky to have grown up in a less complicated time, believing that if you did things the right way — if you played hard, kept your eye on the ball, and got up when you were knocked down — things would turn out all right in the end; and even if they didn't, you could walk away with your head held high. Lucky to have had role models like Somma and his longtime deputy, Paul Milza. And as his friend Vic Esposito was fond of saying, if you grew up in a house where there was food, and love, what else did anybody really need?

There was salt and pepper in his close-cropped beard, and a weariness in his stride that hadn't been there when he was a three-sport athlete in high school and college. But Avena was a football coach, like the man in the casket ... *because* of the man in the casket. He was the one who went back to coach at New Dorp after Somma and Milza retired, and stayed until he could pass the torch to another of Somma's guys.

The older he got, and the more Avena saw of human nature, the more his appreciation grew for the humble man who changed the course of so many lives ... his included ... and helped turn something as unremarkable as a Thanksgiving Day high school football game into a holiday tradition in the old neighborhood, one that transcended school ties and district lines, even though the same team won every year, so everybody knew how it was likely to turn out.

Anywhere football matters, high school or college, there's one game that matters more than the others. For 40 years in the middle of the last century, the Thanksgiving Day game between New Dorp and Curtis was part rivalry, part high school reunion, part block party, as much a part of life on Staten Island as its namesake ferry. The college kids, home for Thanksgiving, showed up full of themselves and the previous night's beer. For their neighbors, young and old, the ride down Richmond Terrace to Weissglass Stadium ... past Sailors Snug Harbor, the home for indigent merchant seamen, where the old salts sat in the sun, watching the big ships slip down the river toward the open sea ... had the feel of a trip to grandmother's house, where they knew family and friends would be waiting.

Somma and Curtis coach Andy Barberi were as different as any two men could be who went to the same schools, played for the same coaches, and sprang from the same roots.

Somma, tall and reserved to the point of shyness, schooled his teams without cursing or belittling kids, armed with an antique offense and an earnestness that made his players determined not to let him down. His meticulously prepared Single Wing football teams were the blocking-and-tackling embodiment of what became his all-purpose credo ... "the hard way is the easy way" ... one that preached the virtues of preparation, sacrifice, and commitment.

"Like he was teaching us to play the way he lived," one of his players said.

Barberi, short, squat, and spectacularly profane, was two years behind Somma in high school and a year behind him in college; always in Somma's shadow, even the day when he played all 60 minutes against the Seven Blocks, and Somma's name was in all the headlines the next morning.

But at the end of World War Two, when both men were in the service, Barberi got home first, and claimed the only job Somma ever wanted. For him, the game was simpler, more combat than Zen, as unambiguous as a punch in the mouth, and he coached with a combination of physical intimidation and my-way-or-the-highway tough love, always ready to knock some sense into somebody's thick skull, if that's what it took. His answer to every tactical problem, "Get lower, hit harder," was shorthand for Barberi's approach to life. Anything worthwhile he'd ever done, he'd done by charging straight ahead, no matter the odds. And God help the fool who stood in his way.

So the Thanksgiving Day game wasn't just the one that mattered most to them, and to everybody else in that corner of the world. It was the proving ground for their wildly contradictory approaches to something that felt like more than a game; a once-a-year test of everything they held dear.

For one day a year, because of them, that corner of New York City had something in common with all those small towns in the South or the Midwest where the game pulled people together, and gave them an opportunity to feel like part of something bigger than themselves ... even though Staten Island was different than those other places, and it would never feel the same way again.

Avena knew nothing stayed the same forever. Even the Latin funeral mass of his childhood ... *"Requiem aeternam dona eis, Domine"* ... had given way to the jarring sounds of English. But as he sat in St. Clare's that February morning with the pale sunlight streaming through the skylight at the peak of the roof, he couldn't help thinking that the church, and the sidewalk outside, and the whole block could've been full of people who had every reason to feel the way he did about Sal Somma.

When it came time for the pallbearers to do their somber duty, Dennis Tancredi took his place alongside the casket. Tancredi, a lifelong runner, still looked trim enough to be the wingback in Somma's Single Wing. He looked at the faces of the men to his left and right, and on the other side of the casket. Avena was there, the way Tancredi knew he would be; and Danny Boylan, their teammate on the '59 team.

The other three pallbearers were a few years younger, but almost as familiar. These were men Tancredi had known his whole life, and trusted the way most men would only trust a brother.

"Look at this," he said. "Three from '59, and three from '64."

Then they lifted, together, and started the old coach on his last journey, past the columns of kids from the high school team lining the path from the street to the church, shivering in their game jerseys under the weak winter sun.

And as the day wore on, between the small talk about kids and jobs and golf games, their thoughts kept rushing back to a simpler time, to the man who'd done so much to shape their lives when they hadn't known it was happening … and to that long-ago season that turned out so differently than any of them thought it would, and bound them in ways they couldn't have seen coming.

2
The Wrong Moses

Staten Island was a different place in the Fall of 1959, the way America was a different place before they shot Jack and Bobby Kennedy, and Martin Luther King; before Vietnam, and the War on Poverty and the War on Drugs, and all the other wars that never seemed to go the way we thought they would.

Only more so.

Because on the Island, 1959 was before the Bridge, which changed everything.

It seemed like a good idea at the time. A bridge across the Narrows, the mile-wide tidal strait that separated Staten Island from Brooklyn at their closest point, would make it easier for Staten Islanders to drive their cars into Manhattan, or to Coney Island or Yankee Stadium or the Bronx Zoo. And who wouldn't want that?

The Verrazano-Narrows Bridge, named for the Italian navigator Giovanni da Verrazano, who negotiated the same waters

400 years earlier, was New York City's last great public works project of the 20th Century, and the final piece in urban planner Robert Moses's vision of a network of highways connecting the city to the suburbs.

Designed by Othmar Ammann, whose bridge-building career began half-a-century earlier with the elegant George Washington Bridge linking upper Manhattan to New Jersey, the Verrazano was an engineering marvel ... a project so massive that its two 700-foot suspension towers are angled a few inches farther apart at the top than they are at water level, to account for the curvature of the earth ... and a bargain besides.

All it cost was $320 million, and a way of life.

When they opened the upper roadway in October of 1964, there were celebrations on both sides of the Narrows; even in Bay Ridge, Brooklyn, where there had been bitter opposition from some of the 7,000 people who were uprooted to make way for the approaches to the Bridge.

"You followed the wrong Moses," one of them told New York City Mayor Robert Wagner at a contentious public hearing, and the man's neighbors jumped up to applaud.

On the Staten Island side, where church bells peeled in celebration on "Bridge Day," a carload of young men camped out at the toll plaza for a week, taking turns saving their place at the head of the line, so theirs would be the first car across. The driver, George Scarpelli, paid the toll with a new Kennedy half-dollar. And on a day so raw that governors Nelson Rockefeller of New York and Richard Hughes of New Jersey earned standing ovations by throwing away their prepared speeches, saloonkeeper Jack Demyan and three friends made the crossing in a 1937 Packard open touring car, pausing at the toll booths long enough to share champagne and cake.

Demyan, a larger-than-life character who catered the wedding scene in *The Godfather* and wound up playing a bartender in the movie, never needed an excuse to throw a party, or to join one already in progress. He and his friends drank the champagne; two bemused toll-takers settled for cake.

But if he'd known how the story ended, Demyan might've parked the Packard across the toll lanes, blocking traffic and delaying the inevitable a few minutes longer. Because as his neighbors would soon realize, traffic on the Bridge flowed both ways, and not all those folks on the Staten Island Expressway were zipping across the Island on their way to someplace else.

Some of them got off, and stayed.

In what seemed like no time at all, while New York's other four boroughs and cities across the country were shrinking, Staten Island's population doubled. And if there was some logic to the Island's earlier development — self-sufficient neighborhoods that grew up around commercial main streets — this new wave of growth wasn't anything like that. Builders threw up housing wherever land was available; which, thanks to an absence of any real civic planning, was everywhere.

Where they couldn't build, they dumped. Before it was closed in 2001, the Fresh Kills landfill, repository for the city's refuse, was the world's largest garbage dump, famously visible from outer space. And with every family that abandoned Brooklyn or the Bronx for the relative safety and open spaces of Oakwood or New Springville — with every woodlot turned into townhouses or cookie-cutter two-family homes, and every convenience store or strip mall built to serve them — the Island looked a little bit more like the places the newcomers thought they were leaving behind.

"It's a different world," Jack Demyan would say years later, mourning the hometown he knew.

"The romance is gone."

But before the Bridge, Staten Island was a world apart: a 14-mile-long, 8-mile wide, kite-shaped wedge of volcanic bedrock hugging the New Jersey shoreline, a full five-mile, 25-minute ferryboat ride from Manhattan, and a shorter voyage from Brooklyn. "The Rock," the natives called it, with something resembling pride.

Places like that, where the borders are *borders* ... two rivers, the Arthur Kill and the Kill van Kull, and the harbor ... tend to resist change, to turn inward, and the Island was always more homogenous and more conservative than the metropolis surrounding it.

Sure, technically it was in the city, one of New York's five boroughs; but it wasn't *of* the city. When Staten Islanders talked about "the city," they meant Manhattan; as in, "We're going to the city tomorrow."

On a clear day you could see the big buildings over there, and sense the power of the metropolis, the hum of commerce and the pulse of the nightlife. But none of that intruded on life on the quiet side of the bay any more than the Statue of Liberty, out there sunning herself in the middle of the harbor.

Thousands of Islanders took the ferry to work in the morning and home again at night, the way Bobby Thomson did that afternoon when he hit the most famous home run of them all, the "Shot Heard Round the World" that lifted the New York Giants into the 1951 World Series, and broke Dodger fans' hearts.

After the game, Thomson took a cab from the Polo Grounds to CBS's Studio 52 in midtown, where he'd agreed in the euphoria of a beery clubhouse celebration to make a live appearance on the Perry Como Show. Then he took the ferry home, caught another taxi to the red brick firehouse on Hannah Street where his brother Jim — who loaned Bobby his spikes the first time he was asked to play with the older men at Clove Lakes Park — was on duty, and spent the rest of his life wondering what all the fuss was about.

The Staten Island where Thomson grew up and Sal Somma's and Andy Barberi's lives kept intersecting was a small town, or a bunch of small towns, some of them dating back to the original Dutch settlements. Stapleton. West Brighton. Port Richmond. New Dorp. Great Kills. Tottenville. They were real neighborhoods ... places where the butcher knew his customers by name, and people cared about their neighbors ... fanning out from St. George on the North Shore, where the ferries docked.

The seat of local government, Borough Hall, was in St. George, across the street from the ferry terminal, along with the central Post Office, and the stately St. George Theater up on Hyatt Street, the first building in the neighborhood to get central air-conditioning, where a white-haired matron patrolled the children's section during Saturday matinees, on the lookout for spitballs or other contraband. A few blocks away, Thomson's alma mater, Curtis High School ... the first public building erected in New York City after the consolidation of the five boroughs ... sat like a castle on the hill, its white Gothic towers visible from far out in the bay.

Toward the southern end of the Island the landscape was greener and less crowded, the streets more like country lanes, until it was almost all woods and open spaces where you could still trap muskrat in the salt marshes, and even those families who didn't have chickens or rabbits in the backyard could go for a Sunday drive without seeing a stoplight.

That Staten Island was a place where parents didn't worry when their children went out to play, as long as they were home when the street lights came on. It was a place where nothing much of consequence to the rest of the world had happened since John Adams, Benjamin Franklin and Edward Rutledge, representatives of the upstart Continental Congress, were rowed across the river from New Jersey in September of 1776 — two months after the Declaration of Independence, and a few weeks after the British routed George Washington's rag-tag army at the Battle of Long Island — to meet with England's Admiral Lord Richard Howe.

The British commander was backed by the most powerful expeditionary force in the history of the Empire; 30,000 British troops were bivouacked on Staten Island and Long Island, and so many warships rode at anchor in the harbor that Washington's soldiers speculated they could've walked from one shore to the other, stepping from deck to deck, without getting their feet wet. But the admiral was no fan of needless bloodshed. Over a luncheon of cold ham, tongue, and mutton, he tried his gentlemanly best to persuade his guests — who in Howe's eyes were Englishmen like himself — to call a halt to the foolish talk of independence, and allow themselves to be welcomed back into the protective embrace of Mother England.

"I feel for America as a brother," Howe told them, "and if America should fall, I should feel and lament it like the loss of a brother."

"My Lord," Franklin responded, "we will use our utmost endeavor to save your Lordship that mortification."

In the centuries that followed, the Island settled toward its role as "the forgotten borough," a place where civil service ambitions went to die for lack of exercise. It wasn't just artistic license in the old movies when some corrupt ward boss would warn an overeager cop suspected of sticking his nose where it didn't belong, "I'll have you walking a beat on Staten Island." Not even Ralph Cramdon, Jackie Gleason's character on *"The Honeymooners,"* wanted to drive a bus route on Staten Island.

More than anything, the Island was defined by its isolation; its Island-ness.

"Before they built the Bridge, you knew everybody, or you knew his brother," Charlie Romanolo, one of Sal Somma's football players, said in a Yogi Berra-like burst of you-know-what-he-meant logic. And on days when the whole neighborhood got together — at the Memorial Day Parade down Victory Boulevard; or on Thanksgiving morning, when everybody went to watch the high school kids from Curtis and New Dorp play football — it seemed to have more in common with Manhattan, Kansas, than it did with the other, more famous, Manhattan across the bay.

"Farmers," they called the New Dorp kids in 1949, when Somma took them to Brooklyn on the 69th Street Ferry to play Lincoln. And they weren't that far from the truth.

On that Staten Island, the one before the Bridge, truck farms and riding trails were as familiar a part of the landscape as the office buildings on Bay Street in St. George, or the shipyards along the Kill van Kull. Down on the South Shore, the orphans at Mount Loretto tended the last herd of dairy cows in New York City. And when the neighborhood kids got together to play pick-up games at Aquehonga Field, not far from the Conference House where Ben Franklin and Lord Howe talked politics at the crossroads of empire and revolution, some of them came barefoot.

The games were different, too, in the days before SportsCenter, Personal Seat Licenses, and participation trophies for 5-year-olds playing tee-ball; before the athletes were chest-thumping millionaires who played to the cameras, and pumped themselves full of steroids meant for horses and who-knows-what-else, growing cartoon muscles and creating a world where nobody could ever be sure if it was safe to believe what they were seeing.

Before television and the big money changed everything, a college scholarship meant a chance at a free education, not a stepping stone to a sneaker contract. Even the pros, who took the games more seriously than they took themselves, were working stiffs like the rest of us; regular people who lived in the neighborhood.

After Bobby Thomson hit the most famous home run in baseball history, 11-year-old Wally Kaner and a few of his friends walked up to the six-room house on Flagg Place where Thomson still lived with his mother, and knocked on the door.

No, Elizabeth Thomson told them, her son hadn't gotten home

yet. But why didn't they come in, have some cookies, and take a look at some of his trophies?

Men like that were grateful not to be stuck in the mill or the mines, or working on the Staten Island docks; and when their playing days were over, they went out and got real jobs. It never would've occurred to them to pound their chests after making a tackle, or dance in the end zone after scoring a touchdown — wasn't that what they were *supposed* to do? — or to stand at home plate and admire their handiwork after hitting a home run.

Mickey Mantle, who hit them farther and more often than anybody in those years, hobbled around the bases after a homer with his head down, as if he was embarrassed to have caused such a fuss, and would just as soon get back to the anonymity of the dugout.

"Act like you've been there before," Lombardi told his Green Bay Packers when they scored a touchdown; and they did.

Modesty ... which, as the sportswriter W.C. Heinz would observe a few years later, doesn't play well on television ... was still in style.

In 1959, when baseball was still the national pastime, a phone call to National Football League headquarters in Philadelphia was likely to be answered by commissioner Bert Bell himself. But seismic change was in the air. NFL owners were still giddy over the Colts' sudden-death overtime victory against the Giants in the 1958 league championship, a game that signaled a shift in the sports landscape, and the start of a partnership with television and Madison Avenue that would soon give the NFL the gravitational pull of a small planet.

New Yorkers, accustomed to having three baseball teams to call their own, were still reeling from the treachery of Walter O'Malley, who hauled the Dodgers off to California, and pulled the Giants along in their wake. But the city still had the Yankees, who counted their World Series checks as a regular supplement to their middle-class salaries, and pity the scrub who didn't do his part. It still had the football Giants of Frank Gifford and Sam Huff, who owned the town once the World Series was over, operating from their unofficial headquarters at Toots Shor's midtown saloon. And any high school kid with 50 cents and a student ID could walk up to the box office at the old Madison Square Garden and get a balcony seat to see the Celtics run past the Knicks in an NBA doubleheader, or watch Gordie Howe elbow the Rangers into submission.

Television hadn't gotten around to hijacking sports and moving the biggest games of the season to the middle of the night, when kids and senior citizens and working people were fast asleep. The few games that were televised were mostly in black and white, preserving a little of the wonder for the first time a kid walked out of the tunnel and into the light at a big-league ballpark, where the grass always seemed a little greener, the dirt a little darker, the bases whiter than white.

Back in the old neighborhood, as Tip O'Neill would famously say about politics, all sports were local.

Sure, a baseball fan who lived on Staten Island might take the ferry and the No. 4 train to the Bronx once a year to see a Yankee game, the way he might take his wife to a Broadway show on their anniversary, or go Christmas shopping at Macy's in Herald Square. But he was just as likely to walk over to Clove Lakes Park or drive out to Reinhardt's Oval on the Island's rural South Shore, where he could watch players like Jerry Stoutland, Billy Cali or Sonny Logan, neighborhood guys who had been "away," taking their shot in baseball's minor leagues, and were back playing in the Sunday morning men's leagues.

Logan's baseball memories were richer than most. He grew up in Sandy Ground, an enclave settled before the Civil War by freed black oystermen from Maryland's Eastern Shore, and he was tutored in the finer points of the game by Herb White, one of a long line of Yankee catchers who found themselves stacked up in the minor leagues behind Hall of Famers Bill Dickey and Yogi Berra. In the summer of 1950, before his senior year in high school, Logan played for the New York Black Yankees.

Three seasons after Jackie Robinson broke baseball's color barrier, the best black players were already gravitating to the big leagues, taking the fans with them, and the Negro Leagues were dying. Logan got there just in time to play against Buck O'Neill and Hall of Famer Oscar Charleston, and to get a hit off Satchel Paige, who theatrically honed his mythic control by substituting a matchbook cover for home plate when he warmed up.

Grown-ups hadn't gotten around to mucking up kids' games, over-scheduling and over-organizing their lives in their eagerness to take all the adversity out of an experience where part of the intrinsic value, if there is any, is in learning to get back up after you've been knocked down. Most parents were too busy doing grown-up things, like work, to spend their evenings and weekends lobbying coaches for playing time, yelling at umpires, or rolling in the dirt with some other kid's father, all in the name of sticking up for their children.

Nobody took Logan, Stoutland, or Cali by the hand to sign them up for Little League or soccer, or biddy basketball; and nobody had to bribe them with trophies or fancy uniforms, or post-game trips to McDonald's. In a world with no Internet or video games, where kids went outside to find their friends and their fun, they played for the unadulterated pleasure of hitting and running and sliding in the dirt, and the satisfying feel of a high fly smacking into the pocket of a hand-me-down glove. When they were old enough, and thought they might be good enough, they tried out for one of the neighborhood sandlot teams, where the coach was a lifer, not some father trying to make his kid a star.

Until then, there were plenty of open fields or vacant lots where kids were allowed to be kids, growing their athletic instincts and their social skills in endless pick-up games of their own invention; choosing up sides, making up the rules as they went along, and settling arguments the same way kids had been doing it forever.

And if that meant they used pieces of cardboard for bases, or somebody occasionally got his nose bloodied ... that was all part of growing up, too.

"We played ball all day," Sonny Logan would say years later, when he was retired from the New York City sanitation department and tending to the playing fields at Wagner College, where visiting coaches remarked that the baseball team had the best-manicured infield in the Northeast Conference.

"What could be better than that?"

Maybe it was only in a climate like that, where kids were allowed to be kids, and guys played ball just for the love of it ... where the first place people looked for entertainment was in their own backyard, and they knew when to stand up and cheer without an electronic message board commanding "GET LOUD!" ... that a high school football game could become the biggest event on the local calendar, even though the same team always won.

The Great Depression, coupled with the cost of outfitting teams in a sport that left so many young boys bloodied, or worse, decimated high school football programs in New York City, and some never recovered. There were five public high schools on Staten Island in the fall of 1959, and three private schools with all-male or coed student bodies, but only two schools that fielded football teams, and one game that mattered.

John Pecoraro was 13 when he saw his first Curtis-New Dorp game. Years later, as a high school coach and athletic director, he'd follow the games from a different perspective. But as he climbed the wooden bleachers that Thanksgiving morning at Weissglass Stadium, where the end zones were nothing more than a few shovelfuls of dirt thrown over the asphalt track where they raced junker stock cars in the warmer months, Pecoraro was amazed to see so many people there, and so many familiar faces.

"It seemed like everybody I knew was there," he said.

"I just assumed that everybody on Staten Island was at that game."

3

Stapes

Sal Somma and Andy Barberi, high school and college teammates before they were coaching adversaries, didn't invent the idea of a backyard rivalry that would keep Thanksgiving dinner waiting on tables all over Staten Island.

Dan Blaine was ahead of them on that one, the way he was ahead of a lot of people at a time when pro football was still a violent novelty, a poor cousin to the college game, and there was room in the start-up National Football League for small-town teams like the Canton Bulldogs, the Pottsville Maroons, and the Staten Island Stapletons, who took their name from the harborside neighborhood straddling the railroad tracks on the Island's east shore.

The Stapes played their home games in Thompson's Stadium, the kind of place that inspired the term "bandbox," built by the owner of the lumberyard around the corner. On a good day, Blaine could shoehorn as many as 10,000 paying customers inside the stockade fence, and into stands meant to seat a few thousand less. On the bad days — and there were plenty of those in the four tumultuous seasons the Stapes were part of the NFL — sometimes there were almost as many people watching for free, from the hillside looming beyond the south end zone, as there were in the wooden bleachers that hugged the field.

"I don't want to say it was small time," New York Giant owner Wellington Mara would say on the other end of a lifetime in pro football, because he was too much of a gentleman to bad-mouth another man's franchise, even one long since dead.

"It was certainly different," Mara said. "The way the stands came up to the sideline, you were always right in the crowd.

"It was a lot more exciting than the Polo Grounds or some other places."

Mara spent most of his life in the family business, growing into his role as patriarch of the Giants and the conscience of the NFL; a farsighted caretaker who helped grow the league from a mom-and-pop operation into a financial colossus by backing revenue-sharing and a merger with the upstart American Football League, even though the Giants operated in the richest market in the country, and had the most to lose.

"We could have a great team," he said by way of explaining that share-the-wealth business model, "but it wouldn't do us much good if we didn't have anybody to play."

He spent 80 years working the same side of the street, without ever sacrificing his dignity or anybody else's, which only made his words more powerful on those rare occasions when he felt compelled to make a point in the locker room, or at the league meetings.

"When he spoke," his friend Art Rooney, the owner of the Pittsburgh Steelers, said, "nobody else said a word."

Mara was nine years old in 1925, when his father, who wouldn't have known if the ball was blown up or stuffed with feathers, bought an NFL franchise for $500, or $2,500 — no record of the transaction exists, but as the years went on, the smaller number made for an even better story — on the premise that in New York, even an empty storefront was worth that much.

While 17-year-old Jack Mara worked the first-down markers for the team's inaugural home opener at the Polo Grounds, his kid brother spent the first half sitting in the stands, and the second half on the Giant bench with 37-year-old Jim Thorpe. The old Sac and Fox Indian, one of the league's first gate attractions, was playing out the string with the Giants, more than a dozen years after he burst into the national consciousness, first at the Carlisle Indian School and then at 1912 Olympic Games, where King Gustav V of Sweden greeted him on the medal stand by declaring, "You, sir, are the greatest athlete in the world."

After all that time in the late-afternoon shadows of the Polo Grounds, Thorpe went home stiff, a condition he routinely treated by self-medicating with a bottle of bootleg whiskey. The younger Mara went home with the sniffles, which upset his mother.

The following Sunday, at Lizette Mara's suggestion, the home team sat on the sunny side of the field, a mandate that followed the Giants all the way to the New Jersey Meadowlands, where Wellington Mara's sons would one day run the team, and one of his 40 grandchildren would sometimes sing the national anthem. It was there at Giants Stadium, in the office suite where he sometimes napped before practice, a habit he borrowed from Winston Churchill — "If it was good enough for Churchill, I guess it ought to be good enough for me" — that Mara remembered those Thanksgiving Day ferry rides to Staten Island, where visiting teams walked from the train to the tiny wooden stadium, and dressed in an un-insulated shed outside the ballpark.

"When the game was over, the players would run off the field to get to the shower," he said. "There was only one shower, and sometimes there was only enough hot water for the first player who got there.

"To get from that shed to the park you had to walk by a bar, and some of those people could make it tough on a visiting team.

"On the days we beat the Stapes, I used to shudder just thinking about the walk back."

But if the facilities left something to be desired, the Stapelton Football Club had a hardcore band of supporters who had followed the team from its semi-pro beginnings. The Stapes once chartered an 18-car special train to carry their fans to a non-league game in Atlantic City. And they had a shrewd leader in Blaine, one of 11 children born and raised right down the block.

Like George Halas of the Chicago Bears and Curly Lambeau of the Green Bay Packers, Blaine was a football player before he was an owner, a hard-nosed halfback when the Stapes were the best semi-pro team around, playing neighborhood rivals like the Montanas, the Imperials, and the Sunnyside Indians in games that were sometimes barely more than legalized fighting. They passed the hat to meet expenses, and split whatever was left over. In the team pictures, Blaine *looks* like a halfback: trim, alert, his body language oozing a cool confidence, like somebody who can't wait for the action to start, with a shock of brown hair falling toward one eye.

The 18th Amendment helped make Blaine a wealthy man, at least by Stapleton standards, in the years after World War One, when Prohibition was the most widely ignored law in the land. All three breweries within a few miles of the ballpark were forced to shift to the production of non-alcoholic ... and less profitable ... beverages, or shutter their doors. But there were rumors you could get a drink with your dinner — or without any dinner at all — at one of Blaine's restaurants.

He poured the untaxed profits into the team, and by the mid-1920s Blaine had managed himself out of a job in the Stapleton backfield, replacing most of the homegrown talent with imported former college players. When a team from Newark waxed the Stapes 33-0, Blaine bought the whole team, outfitting Georgia Tech All-American Doug Wycoff and his Newark teammates in Stapleton's distinctive black jerseys with a white "S" and three white stripes on the sleeves.

By 1928, their last season as an independent, the Stapes were good enough to win three out of four exhibition games against NFL teams, including a 7-0 victory over the Giants, a game in which all eleven Stapleton starters played the entire 60 minutes.

And by opening day in 1929, when all it cost to join the NFL was the promise to field a team, Stapleton had a star.

Scouting was something less than a science in the early days of the league. There was no NFL combine for assessing college players, and no Wonderlic test for probing their psyches; no films to keep coaches working blurry-eyed into the night. If anybody had suggested to Halas or Lambeau that football fans would some-day line up around the block at Radio City Music Hall for the chance to watch NFL executives decide which rookies would play where, they would've laughed until their battle-scarred faces hurt.

By the time he was an undergrad at Fordham, Wellington Mara was a one-man personnel department for the Giants, still so young that when he showed up on the campus of George Washington University to sign Tuffy Leemans, the future Hall of Fame fullback mistook him for an autograph hound. Almost all of what he knew about potential prospects came by word-of-mouth from other players, or from reading the out-of-town newspapers.

But nobody had to tell the Maras about Ken Strong, a unanimous All-American selection at New York University, where he ran for a record 2,100 yards as a senior, and led the country in scoring.

Strong was the whole package: a punishing blocker and fierce defender when he didn't have the football, and the strongest kick-er in the game at a time when pro football was a grind-it-out game of field position. When Grantland Rice, the transplanted Tennessean who invented modern sportswriting, named his all-time college team — "all-time" in this case meaning all of the first half of the 20th century — his halfbacks were Jim Thorpe and Ken Strong.

The NYU football team practiced at Ohio Field in the Bronx, just across the Harlem River from the Polo Grounds, and played most of its home games at Yankee Stadium. When NYU and Fordham met on Thanksgiving, in what the newspapers called "The Battle of the Bronx," the crowds dwarfed anything the pros were drawing.

Until he ruined his wrist running into an outfield wall — and a surgeon compounded the damage, removing a piece of the wrong bone — Strong saw baseball as his best chance to make a living playing a kid's game. The Yankees signed him before he graduated from NYU and sent him to play at New Haven in the Eastern League. He was on his way home from the ballpark one afternoon in August, five weeks before the start of the NFL season, when two young men walked up and introduced themselves as Dan Blaine, owner of the Stapleton Football Club, and his player-coach Doug Wycoff.

Strong explained that the Giants had already contacted him; he had an appointment that same night to meet with Leroy "Bull" Andrews, the Giant coach. But if that was a problem for Blaine, he didn't let on. He gave Strong his phone number, and asked him to call if things didn't work out with the Giants.

Andrews, under instructions from the Maras to get Strong under contract, tried to get him on the cheap. Maybe he thought he was saving the team money, or maybe he figured on recouping some of the savings. Either way, the Giant coach made a mistake that would eventually cost him his job.

If this was how they did business in pro football, Strong could play along. He went straight to a phone and called Blaine, embellishing the Giant offer by a few thousand dollars. By the time they hung up, Strong was the property of the Stapleton Football Club, having agreed to a salary of $5,000 and the promise of a rent-free apartment in St. George, a short walk from the ferry. The Maras read about it in the next day's newspapers.

The NFL Strong joined in 1929 was a world apart from the league he left for good as a player, 18 years later. Pro football was a hard game played by hard, hungry men who came out of the mill towns and off the farms and played both sides of the ball, often for 60 minutes without a rest, without facemasks and sometimes without helmets. And they harbored no illusions about the game ever making them rich.

The Stapes practiced in the evening, to make it easier for players and coaches to get to their day jobs, and scheduling was haphazard. Blaine's team made one western swing each season, to cut down on expenses, and routinely played midweek exhibitions to improve their cash flow. Because no Sunday games were allowed in the Philadelphia neighborhood the Frankford Yellow Jackets called home, visiting teams often played Frankford on a Saturday and the Stapes or the Giants the next day, pulling on the same wet, dirty uniforms for their second game of the weekend.

Even with Strong and Wycoff anchoring the backfield, the Stapes were never better than middle-of-the pack, finishing sixth, sixth, and seventh their first three years in the league, before falling to last place in their final NFL season, in a league that had shrunk along with the economy, from 12 teams to eight.

They had their moments. The Stapes knocked the Giants out of first place with a 7-6 upset in the next-to-last game of the 1930 season, and they held the 1932 Bears, who had two of the biggest stars in the game in Red Grange and Bronko Nagurski, to a scoreless tie. "Probably my proudest moment as a pro," Strong would call it years later. But even then, the home team lost money on the game.

When Blaine asked the league for permission to suspend operations for the 1933 season, Wycoff and some of the others stayed to play a schedule of independent opponents, losing all five of their exhibitions against NFL teams, and more of the owner's money. Strong left to join the Giants for $250 a game, a steep cut from what the Stapes were paying him.

He led the league in scoring in 1933, and helped the Giants win a title the next year, scoring a championship-game record 17 points in the famous "Sneakers Game" against the Bears, when the Giants changed footwear at halftime to compensate for a frozen field. At the age of 38 he came out of retirement to become one of pro football's first kicking specialists before quitting for good three years later, as the Giants' all-time leading scorer. But not before the afternoon in 1944 when he jogged into the Giant huddle, late in a one-sided game against the Redskins, and turned to a puzzled Tuffy Leemans, who was calling the plays.

"How about letting the old man carry the ball?"

It took Leemans a few seconds to find his voice.

"Are you nuts?"

"My son's in the stands," Strong said. "He's never seen me run."

The first time they gave him the ball, the hole closed before he could get there, and Strong was thrown for an ugly loss. On the next play he found a seam off tackle and fell forward for a five-yard gain, the last gasp in an historic career.

The old Stape was a proud man, not given to sentiment when it came to the business of pro football. But his voice was husky when he got back to the huddle.

"Thanks, Tuffy," he said. "I just ended my career as a running back."

In retrospect, Dan Blaine's' NFL adventure was probably

doomed from the start. The old ballpark was so small that even when every seat was sold, by the time the visiting team collected its guarantee, there was little left over. And it was Blaine's bad luck that the Stapes made their NFL debut three weeks before Black Tuesday, the day the New York Stock Exchange crashed, signaling the start of the Great Depression.

By 1932, as the Depression deepened, the full-house crowds had melted away. Only 4,500 diehards saw the Stapes and Giants play to a bitter tie on Thanksgiving. Even fewer braved the cold to watch the season finale against the defending champion Packers and their brilliant but undomesticated halfback John McNally, who borrowed his pro football alias, Johnny Blood, from the title of a Rudolph Valentino silent movie, *Blood and Sand*.

Last call for pro football in Stapleton.

After playing as an independent in 1933, Blaine got permission to suspend league operations again the following season, but this time he didn't have the energy or the resources to field a team. By the summer of 1935 the Stapleton franchise was declared forfeit, and Staten Islanders were left with their memories, and the afterglow of those Thanksgiving afternoons when the Giants had to walk the gauntlet from their locker room to the field, and back again after the game, to a cold shower.

For the four seasons the Stapes were in the league, the two big Thanksgiving Day rivalries in the NFL were the Chicago Cardinals and Chicago Bears… and Giants-Stapes. And because the college boys at Fordham and NYU had first call on the big-city ballparks, and on the loyalties of the sporting press, and the public, the pros played every Thanksgiving on Staten Island.

The Stapes won two of the four holiday games, including the 1930 upset that cost the Giants a share of the league championship, and tied a third.

But there was no Thanksgiving Day game in Stapleton quite like the first one.

Thanksgiving, 1929, dawned raw and cold, bad news for Blaine, who had already lost one payday to the weather that fall. It rained for a time, then the rain turned to snow flurries, as temperatures dropped by the hour. But by early afternoon the skies had cleared, and more than 10,000 ticketholders, bundled into greatcoats and in some cases fortified by flasks of bootleg whiskey to ward off the chill, pushed their way inside the stockade fence, squeezing close to their neighbors to make room for one more, and one more after that.

The overflow filled the nearby hillside.

Out west, the Bears-Cardinals game was no contest, as Hall-of-Famer Ernie Nevers scored all six touchdowns in a 40-6 Cardinal rout for bragging rights in the Windy City.

Right from the start, Giants-Stapes was more contentious. The first time the Giants had the ball, Strong tackled Giant end Ray Flaherty along the sideline, and their momentum carried them toward the low wire fence that separated players from spectators. Flaherty, a veteran of the give-no-quarter, ask-no-quarter rough-and-tumble of the pro game, jumped up ready to fight.

"When the whistle blew," Strong remembered years later, "Ray looked up and saw an old lady leaning over the fence, waving an umbrella.

"She'd been hitting him on the head, and he thought I was reaching up and punching him."

The home team gave the big crowd something to cheer about, rallying from a two-touchdown deficit before the Giants, who keyed on Strong whenever the Stapes had the ball, padded their lead with a late touchdown on a fake field goal, to win 20-7.

But the Stapes and Giants didn't have the holiday, or the ballpark, all to themselves.

Earlier that morning, in the worst of the weather, almost 5,000 fans filled the same bleachers to watch the kids from Curtis High School play Augustinian Academy, the little Catholic school from just over the hill.

Enrollment at Augies barely exceeded 100 boys, half of them seminarians preparing for the priesthood. But in an era when high school football existed at the whim of skittish administrators who wondered how such a violent game fit into the educational template, coach Joe Baeszler, a former Stape from the semi-pro years, had forged a formidable team; and the two schools had a history. Legend had it that shortly after the turn of the century, students at Curtis and Augies arranged a football game for the right to wear maroon and blue as their school colors. More than a century later, Augies alumni were quick to notice that Curtis teams still wore maroon and *white*. And the 1929 game was played against the backdrop of the Academy's surprise victory in 1925, and scoreless ties the two years after that.

In the last minute of the '29 game, while the Giants were making their way to Staten Island by ferry, Curtis was protecting a 12-7 lead, built on the strength of a fourth-quarter touchdown by captain Bill Shanahan, who would soon be headed for college stardom at Penn.

But the Curtis kids got careless, or they got greedy. Trying to pad their margin of victory, they went to the air, always a shaky proposition, even in good weather, in the days when the football was shaped like a watermelon, and was often just as slippery. Augies captain Joie Wright intercepted Shanahan's pass at his own 30-yard line, and for a few adrenaline-fueled seconds it looked like he might take it back all the way, and turn the game on its ear.

Shanahan couldn't catch Wright. One of the Curtis ends, Fred DeSio, came from the other side of the field and caught him inside the 20, and time expired before the Augies could run another play. It was an ending so breathless, so full of what-might-have-been, it would've been easy for the cold and wet eyewitnesses to forget the first touchdown of the day, a quick burst up the middle by the Curtis fullback, a hard-running newcomer named Sal Somma.

4

Pelicans and Cyclones

By any measure, Al Fabbri, the Curtis High School football coach in the 1920s and 30s, was a formidable figure. Everything about him, from the powerful shoulders to the thick, black mustache, broadcast a sense of purpose. Even his stiff-legged gait recalled tales of a younger Fabbri who allegedly used the spine of an umbrella as a makeshift splint, and finished a game on a broken leg.

But when he limped up the front steps of the big house on Simonson Avenue, bent on persuading Anthony Somma to let his son quit a perfectly good job in the Baltimore & Ohio Railroad machine shop so he could go back to school and play a boy's game on Saturday afternoons, Fabbri knew he had his work cut out for him.

"It wasn't easy," Mary Somma Koffer was saying almost 80 years later, sitting in the same kitchen where Fabbri negotiated with her mother and father for her brother's future. Just outside the kitchen window, her father's initials were still visible where he drew them in the cement at the base of a flight of steps, a few years after the family moved in: "A.S., 1931."

A few months shy of her 100th birthday, Koffer suffered from a degenerative disk condition that made it difficult for her to get up and down, or climb stairs. But the years hadn't stolen her memory, or her relentless good humor.

"Sal had it hard," she said. "My father expected too much from his boys."

Like millions of other European immigrants who streamed through Ellis Island at the end of the 19th and the early part of the 20th Centuries, Anthony and Elizabeth Somma came to America looking for the Land of Opportunity, and found hard work, and even harder times.

They found both in the railroad town of Ridgeley, West Virginia, perched on a narrow spit of sandstone in a horseshoe bend of the Potomac, where the river's South Branch winds through the Allegheny Mountains, serving as a natural boundary between West Virginia and Maryland.

Anthony Somma worked in the Western Maryland Railway shop. With eight children to feed, he and his wife managed to make ends meet by taking in boarders, most of them recent Italian immigrants like themselves, in a house with no running water; and by selling canned goods from the shelves of what passed for a country store. When they baked in the outdoor brick oven, the coal miners would come down from the hills to buy bread, and every now and again one of them went away with a jar of Anthony's homemade wine.

Even then, the Sommas lived hand-to-mouth. One of Sal's chores as a boy was to walk the railroad right-of-way with a burlap bag, picking up stray pieces of coal to burn for heat or cooking fuel, a job he sometimes expedited by setting up empty cans on a fence alongside the tracks, where the firemen and brakemen on passing freights couldn't resist using them for target practice, pitching coal from their tender.

There were nights he went to bed hungry, and days when all he had to eat was some homemade mayonnaise slathered on a slice of homemade bread. Years later, as an adult, Sal would only put mustard on a sandwich; the sight of a jar of mayonaisse was enough to rekindle unhappy memories, and roil his perpetually nervous stomach.

His father ran a tight ship. Anthony Somma wanted his children to wear shoes, but in the summer they often went barefoot along the banks of the Potomac, fishing or swimming until they heard the switch engine coming down the tracks at the end of the work day.

"Poppa's coming!" somebody would yell, and they'd grab soap and run to wash their feet at the ice house just upstream where a clay pipe discharged hot water into the river, anxious to get into their shoes before their father saw them, and used his belt on them for being disobedient.

Out there between the river and the mountains, there was plenty of room for a boy to grow; and if he got bored — and he was daring enough — he could hop a slow-moving freight and ride 30 or 40 miles over the mountains, through some of the most spectacular scenery east of the Rockies. In the evening, he'd ride another train home.

But life on the Potomac wasn't all fishing and swimming and running barefoot through the woods, or seeing the sights. In a region where jobs were scarce even before the Depression, newcomers didn't always feel welcome. The Somma girls learned not to wear earrings in a part of the country where pierced ears marked them as foreigners.

"They called us guineas," Mary Koffer said, the hurt still catching in her throat.

Worse yet, thugs who spoke their own language wanted to steal from them. The Black Hand, more notorious in big cities like New York than in rural West Virginia, was more a method than an organization; a crude form of extortion in which the local gangsters — many of them petty criminals back in the Old Country — demanded protection money, and threatened violence if they weren't paid.

In that dirt-poor corner of West Virginia, the bandits didn't ask for much; a dollar now, a few more later. But Anthony Somma worked too hard to give away what little he had. There were times when Sal, not yet a teenager, took his turn sitting up through the night with a rifle in his lap, for fear somebody would burn the house down around the Sommas while they slept.

And every spring, when the snows melted upstream, the river came for them.

"We lived in the gully, with the mountains all around us," Mary said. "The water would come into the house, right up to the bedrooms. We had two boats ... a canoe and a flat-bottomed boat. When the river came up, we'd go up onto the mountain until the water went down again.

"Then we had to get rid of the mud."

The worst of the floods, in the spring of 1924, swept away bridges, scattered freight cars like children's toys, and left three-quarters of the town under water. For weeks afterward, the Sommas ate from rusting cans, their labels peeled away by the receding floodwaters, never knowing until they opened a can if they were having peaches for dinner that night, or beef stew.

Elizabeth Somma might've been new to the neighborhood, but she had no intention of spending the rest of her life shoveling mud out of her kitchen; especially not in a place where the neighbors called her children ugly names, and bandits from the Old Country wanted to steal her family's hard-earned money.

She had a sister on Staten Island, and when Elizabeth took the train to New York she saw her relatives had indoor plumbing instead of a "back house." There were jobs for anybody who wasn't afraid of hard work, and the neighborhood was full of recent immigrants. When she walked the streets of Rosebank or Clifton, a lot of the accents she heard were similar to her own.

"In West Virginia," Mary Koffer said, "all we had was the railroad and the mines. My mother had five sons. She didn't want them to wind up in the mines."

Her husband, having already abandoned his native Naples for a strange and sometimes hostile land, wasn't inclined to pick up and move again; but it wouldn't be the last time he lost an argument in his own kitchen. Elizabeth and a few of the older children went north first. And when the Western Maryland went out on strike, the rest of the family followed them to Staten Island.

The Sommas settled in Clifton, wedged between the larger communities of Rosebank, a heavily Italian neighborhood where nationalist Giuseppe Garibaldi lived in exile when there was a price on his head in Europe, and Stapleton, where Dan Blaine's Stapes played football. There they were within walking distance of the Baltimore and Ohio machine shop, where Anthony Somma and his oldest son John found work.

They rented at first, before moving into the big house on Simonson Avenue, built by relatives of Cornelius Vanderbilt, the railroad and shipping tycoon who got his start ferrying passengers and freight between Staten Island and Manhattan — the original Staten Island ferry. It was once a grand residence, with 12-foot ceilings and 24 rooms, enough for all the servants when the original owners were in residence, and a view of the water all the way to the Narrows, where the harbor opened to the sea.

Eighty years later, when the Sommas arrived on Staten Island from West Virginia, the property had been abandoned; the yard was overgrown, the house left to the mercy of the weather, and vandals. Anthony and Elizabeth scraped together what little money they had, sold some property being held for them in Italy, and bought it for $4,000. Their neighbors, men accustomed to working with their hands, pitched in to make it livable.

Not everybody in the family was happy to be on Staten Island. One time or another, each of the boys, uprooted from the only life they'd known, ran off. Most of the time they went back to the little railroad town on the banks of the Potomac, and stayed until their money ran out; then they came home.

If there were early signs that Sal, the fourth of Anthony and Elizabeth's eight children, was destined to become a legendary figure in their adopted hometown ... a symbol of up-from-nothing achievement and quiet integrity, and role model to generations of high school football players ... the Sommas missed them. At the start of the next school year, they enrolled him in classes at Curtis High School.

"I hated it," he said. "There was no way I was going to stay." After the third day he came home from school, packed a change of clothes, and left to find his own way in the world.

He was 16.

He wound up in Harrisburg, Pa., with nowhere to stay and no money to go on. After spending two nights in a pool hall to escape the cold, he walked into a recruiting station and enlisted in the Army, identifying himself as Anthony Chapell, a made-up name that lacked the flair of John McNally's football alias, Johnny Blood, but was good enough to satisfy a lazy recruiting sergeant.

"I was big for my age," Somma said years later. "I don't know where I got the name. I must've read it somewhere.

"Maybe the recruiter hadn't met his quota that month, so he took me."

Afraid to communicate with his brothers and sisters — even Mary, who was closest to Sal in age, and his staunchest ally — he couldn't resist writing to Roy Boatman, a boyhood friend in West Virginia. Word got around in Ridgeley, the way it often does in a small town, especially one with a pool hall, and it was only a matter of time until the news reached Staten Island.

A cousin, Tony Bona, was sent to investigate, and found Sal cleaning the mules for a machine-gun company at Fort Jay on Governors Island, right out there in the middle of the New York harbor, within sight of Staten Island. After months of mucking out stalls, the novelty of life in the military had worn off.

"Boy," Somma told his cousin, "am I glad to see you."

With the help of friends who had a better command of English, and of the way things worked in their adopted country, Anthony Somma appealed to the Army for his son's release.

"I wish to withdraw Selvan Somma (my son) from the U.S. Army, on the plea of non-consent and minority," he wrote to Captain J.P. Nolan, Sal's company commander.

"I positively affirm that I knew nothing of his actions or whereabouts until recently, when, through friends of his, I was informed of his location.

"I am the father of a large family and ask his release because my present income is not sufficient to assure a comfortable living."

With no war to be fought, and none on the horizon in the winter of 1927, the Army had little need for under-age recruits using assumed names.

A few weeks later the chastened runaway was back on Staten Island, and put to work alongside his father and older brother, as an apprentice mechanic in the B&O shop down the street.

Football was his salvation. All the Somma boys loved sports, football in particular, and Sal most of all; and the game loved him back. He was almost six feet tall, and growing into his big hands and feet; back in West Virginia, the job of mashing grapes for wine fell to him, because his father said Sal had the biggest feet in the family. He liked the freedom he found on the football field, and he liked the contact. Out there, where you were only limited by your ability and your willingness to run, and hit, and knock people down — or knock them out — nobody called him "guinea."

Out there, he was as good as anybody.

The memory of it made his sister smile.

"Sal loved football," she said. "Football was his life."

And he could play. Word of his prowess got around, and it wasn't long before he was playing for the Fort Wadsworth Pelicans, one of the better men's teams on the Island at a time when every neighborhood had a football and baseball team to call its own, or it had two.

The crowd stood three deep on both sidelines when the Pelicans traveled to the other side of the Island to play the Heberton Cyclones, one of the few teams to beat them the previous season, in a rivalry that always seemed one punch shy of outright mayhem.

Twice in the first half, the Cyclones drove deep into Pelican territory, but couldn't score. In the second half the Pelicans took over, punching home the game's first touchdown at the start of the fourth quarter, and tacking on another in near darkness. Somma was in the middle of all of it from his position at right end, chasing down Cyclone ballcarriers in the backfield, and throwing cross-body blocks that could be felt from across the field.

When it was over, the Pelican fans rushed the field and tore down the homemade goalposts. Then they piled into their cars, honking horns and making a spectacle of themselves all the way back to Fort Wadsworth, with the players riding on the running boards in their bright orange uniforms. And a few weeks after that, Al Fabbri came knocking on the Sommas' door.

From Monday to Saturday, Fabbri was the football coach at Curtis High School. On Sundays, he coached the Cyclones; but he was always on the lookout for younger men who might still have some schooling to do, and could help the high school team.

In his first few years at Curtis, Fabbri's teams struggled. But by 1928 the White Warriors shut out eight of their nine opponents, and their young coach planned on doing a lot more winning. The new kid from West Virginia, who was such a disruptive force when the Pelicans beat Fabbi's Cyclones, was a big part of those plans.

Anthony Somma wasn't easily moved. Like a lot of immigrants, he came to America with a built-in distrust of government, and authority. Experience taught him that when push came to shove, all a man could depend on was family, and too much education seemed like one more way to divide the family unit. When Rose Somma, the oldest of Sal's three sisters, finished high school back in West Virginia and wanted to go on to nursing school, her father dug in his heels; Rose went to work in the Kelly Springfield tire plant across the river in Cumberland, Md., and never got back to school. And now Sal, who was young and strong, and already had a paying job, wanted to throw it away to play football?

That mindset wasn't uncommon. Especially among the tight-knit Italian families of Rosebank and Clifton, the attitude that boys of a certain age should get a job and help put food on the table ... and that college was for somebody else's kids ... passed from one generation to the next.

"The joke used to be if you didn't work on the docks, you must be a bookmaker," John Pecoraro, whose father *was* a bookmaker, remembered years later.

Times were hard, and getting harder, the elder Somma told Fabbri in his broken English. He hadn't gone to the trouble of tracking down his wayward son and prying him from the Army's hands, just so Sal could play some schoolboy game.

He was only one man, Anthony said, and the family needed the extra money his son was bringing home.

Down at the Baltimore & Ohio machine shop, Sal was making 27 cents an hour.

Fabbri, whose own parents were from the Old Country, appealed to Anthony Somma in their native tongue. If Sal played high school football, the coach might be able to find him a college scholarship. It wouldn't cost the Sommas anything for him to go to school. And with a college degree, Sal would be better equipped to help support the family.

"In America l'educazione è la chiave per il future. Senza l'educatione non c'è niente il figlio. Con la scuola, tutto sta aperto per lui."

"In America, education is the key to the future. Without an education, there's nothing for your son.

"With schooling, everything is open for him."

The coach leaned closer, his fists resting on Anthony Somma's kitchen table, his eyes locked on those of the railroad man from Appalachia.

"Antonio ... è d'onore, peri nostril, per noi Italian."

"It's a matter of pride, for our own, for us Italians!"

"Thank God, Fabbri spoke Italian," Mary Koffer was saying in the kitchen where the deal was struck.

"Sal would've wound up working down at the B&O forever."

5

A Man Among Boys

Sal Somma wasn't the first dropout Al Fabbri coaxed back to school — and onto the football field — or the last star he recruited off the sandlots when he was building something out of nothing at Curtis High School, the way Somma would do it a few decades later at New Dorp.

Walter Scholl was a few months shy of graduation at Port Richmond High School the first time Fabbri saw him play in a sandlot game.

Scholl was a little bit of a kid; 150 pounds of gristle, strung over a 5-8 frame. But he could run, and he could throw — he played baseball and ran track at Port Richmond, one of those schools that dropped football in the early years of the Depression — and when he had a football under his arm, the little guy had a gift that couldn't be learned, or taught: he made people miss.

Fabbri presented Scholl a radical proposal: drop out of school for the spring semester, delay his high school graduation, play football at Curtis in the fall, and Scholl could earn himself a college scholarship.

Viewed through a 21ˢᵀ Century prism, the story smacks of scandal, the kind of blatant recruiting that could get a high school coach fired; but for a kid whose best hope in the middle of the Depression was to find a job on the docks or in the shipyards, it held the promise of a different kind of life.

In his first high school game, Scholl scored two touchdowns. Two weeks later, 6,000 Staten Islanders watched him run for four touchdowns, return an interception for a fifth, and throw for a sixth score in a 42-0 rout.

A star was born.

Playing for Curtis in the 1930s was like being part of a semi-pro team. The White Warriors played their home games at Thompson's Stadium, drawing crowds that Dan Blaine's Stapes might've envied toward the end of their NFL run. After scuffling through his first few seasons, Fabbri had established Curtis as the dominant high school team in the city, and he didn't have to worry about polishing his record; he scheduled games from Virginia to Massachusetts, lining up the best opponents he could find.

Frank Goodell, an all-city quarterback at Curtis, would go on to play at Pitt. "We could never get any home games," he said. "Fabbri would hear about these teams everybody was talking up, and he'd get them to play us."

When Curtis went to Massachusetts to play Marblehead High in the fall of 1936, more than 500 Staten Islanders made the trip by car, train and the Colonial Line overnight boat to Boston. Back on the Island, hundreds more gathered outside the offices of the local newspaper, where the play-by-play was delivered by Western Union teletype, and relayed over a loudspeaker to the crowd in the street.

The game was a contrast in styles: the power game favored by Fabbri against the deceptive spins, reverses and laterals of Marblehead coach Charlie McGuiness, an ahead-of-his-time maverick who never played football, and didn't believe in letting his players hit between games. McGuiness learned the game in one summer with the legendary Pop Warner, Jim Thorpe's old coach at Carlisle, after Warner moved on to Stanford.

The year before, in a game billed as "the mythical Eastern championship," Marblehead undressed Curtis 29-0, ruining an otherwise perfect season for the Staten Islanders; and the rematch started in similar fashion, with Marblehead scoring on its first two possessions.

Despite the score, Scholl was all over the field, making tackles from sideline to sideline, and a threat to score whenever he touched the ball. In the fourth quarter, Curtis finally got on the scoreboard. Then Scholl fielded a punt at his own 40-yard line, eluded a tackler, and outran everybody for a 60-yard touchdown, cutting Marblehead's lead to 13-12.

The Warriors were back in Marblehead territory, driving for the go-ahead score, when time expired.

"As far as I'm concerned," Fabbri told his disappointed players, "you won today."

Then Charlie McGuiness, the eccentric Marblehead coach who learned the game from old Pop Warner himself, made an unscheduled appearance on the losers' sideline, where he sought out Scholl.

"You should have this," McGuiness said, handing the game ball to the little guy who played so well, for so long, for the losing team.

By season's end, Scholl owned the New York City schoolboy scoring record, and had his choice of college scholarships. He chose Cornell, the start of a family legacy. In the years to come he'd become a war hero — in his first combat mission as a fighter pilot over North Africa, Scholl shot down a German ace — and, later in life, the silver-haired public face of Merrill-Lynch, one of the most powerful firms on Wall Street. So when Fabbri convinced him to postpone his high school graduation so he could play football, he wasn't just changing Walter Scholl's life. He was changing the fortunes of an entire family for generations to come.

Scholl arrived in Ithaca with his only suit in a cardboard suitcase, and a pair of football cleats that were a gift from Fabbri.

By the time he left, he was a cult figure, the sparkplug for Cornell's undefeated1939 team, and the instigator of back-to-back upsets of Big 10 powerhouse Ohio State.

By the time they went to Dartmouth for the next-to-last game of the 1940 season, the Big Red were riding an 18-game unbeaten streak, ranked second in the Associated Press football poll, and in the hunt for a national title.

Playing in snow and sleet, frustrated by the muddy footing and a new defensive scheme drawn up by Dartmouth coach Earl "Red" Blaik — who would go on to greater fame a few years later as Army's wartime coach — Cornell trailed 3-0 in the fourth quarter. Then the Big Red mounted an 11th-hour drive that ended with Scholl throwing to Bill Murphy for the winning touchdown on the last play of the game.

Almost immediately, Dartmouth protested that the winning touchdown pass had come on a "fifth-down" play. But even as the controversy gained traction in Hanover and Ithaca, and Cornell president Edmund Ezra Day told the crowd at a campus rally he didn't want a "long count" victory ... a reference to Gene Tunney's controversial victory over Jack Dempsey in their 1927 heavyweight championship fight ... officials of the Eastern Collegiate Athletic Conference announced that they were powerless to reverse an officiating error once the game was over.

Two days later, Cornell's 16-millimeter films of the game — still a novelty in 1940, when it was considered unsportsmanlike to use game films to scout an opponent — confirmed that the Big Red had benefited from an extra down on the last drive.

Cornell coach Carl Snavely called a team meeting to break the news to his players. And with everything that was on the line ... the win streak, the national ranking, the chance to stamp themselves as the greatest of all Cornell teams ... Cornell gave the victory to Dartmouth, because it was the right thing to do.

If Scholl's running style resembled a river finding its way to the sea, darting this way or that across the landscape, always seeking the path of least resistance, Somma's was that of a man who knew exactly where he was headed, and didn't want to get too far off course. He was a bruising, straight-ahead fullback and tailback, all elbows and knees and a handful to tackle, and a punishing linebacker who could kick an extra point in a pinch.

In the three seasons he played for Fabbri, Curtis lost a total of three games. After using him at end in his first game, Fabbri moved him to the backfield, where Somma was the perfect weapon in the old Bates College lineman's straightforward attack: tough, strong, fast enough and versatile enough to play all four backfield positions, and apparently fearless, never shying away from contact.

By mid-season that first year, he was "Curtis's rising star," according to the local newspaper, "... playing, as he always does, without caring a bit about what injuries he would receive."

By the middle of his second season of high school football, it wasn't uncommon for Somma to account for all the scoring on a Saturday afternoon. In one game against Brooklyn Prep he returned the opening kickoff 85 yards for a touchdown, and took an interception 55 yards for the only other score. In the season finale against Augustinian Academy, he helped ruin any hope for a repeat of the Thanksgiving Day thriller the year before, scoring two of the first three touchdowns before Fabbri cleared his bench in a 44-0 rout.

In his last high school season, Curtis was one of four teams chosen to play in a post-season "tournament" for charity. Somma, one of the Warrior co-captains, was the lone repeater on the *New York American's* all-city team. New York University, Ken Strong's old school, was holding a scholarship for him.

In the team picture, he's the one in the middle, holding the football. Andy Barberi, who would one day be his accomplice, and after that his adversary in the games of their lives, is kneeling in the front row, already a regular, even as a sophomore; a five-by-five bundle of aggression who kept coming, and coming, until the guys on the other side of the ball relented, or got tired of trying to hold him off, and let him through.

Even then, Barberi was the gregarious one; the one most likely to crack a joke in class, or tell his teammates, "Let's kick their asses!" Somma was more reserved; more shy, his classmates thought, than aloof.

And if he sometimes looked and acted like a man among boys, it's because he was.

He was 19 when he played his first high school game, and 22 by the time he graduated in the spring of 1932, voted "Most Popular," "Best Sport," and permanent Class President by his classmates.

The literary quotation alongside his yearbook picture — a composed young man with waves of brown hair pushed back off his forehead — smacks of adolescent hero worship:

"Who're excels in what we prize
Appears a hero in our eyes."

He wasn't the only older player on the Curtis roster, or the only one playing catch-up in the classroom.

The rulebook didn't say much about who could or couldn't play. And in the middle of the Great Depression — when the city's make-work programs put picks and shovels into the smooth hands of unemployed engineers and insurance salesmen, men accustomed to wearing suits and ties to the office — plenty of parents were forced to decide whether a high school diploma for their teenaged son was a luxury the family could afford.

It wasn't unusual for Fabbri's players to have one foot in the classroom and the other in the labor force, extending their high school careers by spending the spring semester working on the docks, and playing football in the fall.

There was no missing Somma's raw athleticism. In his first brush with a new sport, he won the county pole vault championship. But what set him apart was the passion he brought to football, fueled in equal parts by his love for the game and his determination to avoid a lifetime in the Baltimore and Ohio rail yard.

Fabbri changed Somma's world that day in the kitchen of the big house on Simonson Avenue, when the coach appealed to Anthony Somma in his native tongue.

He'd spend most of his adult life repaying that debt, one kid at a time.

Decades later, on those rare occasions when an aging Fabbri stopped by to watch him at work, Somma didn't hide his feelings for the man he considered a second father.

"He loved Fabbri," Larry Ambrosino, who played for Somma in the 1960s, remembered.

"When he came to practice, everything stopped.

"Fabbri would want to show us a 'center-eligible' play or some crazy thing, and we'd be rolling our eyes. But Mr. Somma always made sure we showed him the proper respect."

"It was like the Pope was coming to visit," John Iasparro said.

6
De-emphasized Again

Hal Squier was a busy man in the fall of 1935, when you couldn't watch the games on your high-definition, flat-screen TV or pull them in on your satellite dish, and the only way to see the World Series or the Kentucky Derby or the biggest games of the college football season was to buy a ticket, or wait to watch the newsreels at your neighborhood movie theater.

The only formal training the sports editor of the *Staten Island Advance* could cop to was as a plumber's helper. He was working as a fire insurance inspector when the previous sports editor, John "Ten Flat" Drebinger, left on short notice to take a job as the second-string baseball writer at the *New York Globe*, a move that worked out well for both men.

Drebinger, who jumped from the *Globe* to the *Times* a few months later, covered every World Series from 1929 until 1963, and wound up with his name on a plaque in the writers' wing of the Baseball Hall of Fame. Squier, a frequent visitor to the *Ad-*

vance newsroom, was the next one through the door, and somebody offered him the vacant desk.

Right from the start, he looked the part, with an unlit cigar permanently lodged in one corner of his ready smile; and he knew the turf. What he lacked in education, Squier made up for with a love of the games, and the people who played them. He helped put out the paper six days a week, producing reams of copy on a manual typewriter with a two-fingered hunt-and-peck method of his own invention, running full pages of box scores from local leagues he helped start, and shamelessly promoting every neighborhood event like it was Army-Navy. On Sundays, when there was no paper, he came in late, usually straight from a game.

In 40 years on the job, he never took a vacation.

But there were times when a guy couldn't anchor himself to his desk and still call himself a sportswriter, no matter how devoted he was to the local beat.

In the fall of 1935, with most of the country still mired in the Depression and desperate for something to cheer about, college football served up one riveting match-up after another, each one blown larger-than-life by the cheerleaders in the sporting press; which is how Squier found himself in Columbus, Ohio, the first Saturday in November, watching a kid from the old neighborhood play in a Notre Dame-Ohio State game being billed as "The Battle of the Century."

Bill Shakespeare was a fire captain's son from Westerleigh, a Staten Island neighborhood of neat homes and well-kept lawns; the kind of place where young boys joined the Boy Scouts and minded their manners, and sometimes they went off to play football for Notre Dame.

Four years earlier, Shakespeare met Notre Dame coach Knute Rockne in a chance encounter at a high school awards dinner. Or, at the very least, it was chance on Shakespeare's part. The charismatic Rockne, who invented the institution we call Notre

Dame football, rarely did anything that wasn't calculated.

Until that meeting, Shakespeare planned to go to the University of Alabama, where he would've thrown the ball to Bear Bryant and Don Hutson, a couple of Arkansas farm boys who wound up making some football history of their own. He changed his mind after five minutes with Rockne, who spent most of his adult life convincing young men to do things they hadn't thought about doing – most famously on that Saturday afternoon against Army when he asked the boys to answer the deathbed wish of departed halfback George Gipp and "win just one for the Gipper."

But by the fall of 1935 Rockne was gone, too, killed when his plane went down in a Kansas wheat field a few months before Shakespeare arrived in South Bend.

Death, it seemed, had been an all-too-frequent visitor in the Irish locker room. Joe Sullivan, Shakespeare's first friend at Notre Dame, died of pneumonia in the spring of '35, after being elected captain of the football team for the coming season. As a tribute to Sullivan, the Irish didn't name a successor, and dedicated each game to their dead captain's memory.

Notre Dame was coached by Elmer Layden, part of Rockne's "Four Horsemen" backfield immortalized by Grantland Rice in the most famous newspaper lead of them all:

"*Outlined against a blue-gray October sky, the Four Horsemen rode again. In dramatic lore they are known as Famine, Pestilence, Destruction and Death.*

"*These are only aliases.*

"*Their real names are Stuhldreher, Miller, Crowley and Layden.*"

But Notre Dame-Ohio State wasn't just a big game in Columbus or South Bend, or in the ethnic precincts of Chicago and New York where the Subway Alumni, those legions of loyal fans who had never seen the Golden Dome, rooted from afar, and the nuns who taught elementary school weren't shy about having their students pray for a Notre Dame victory.

Six weeks into the college season, both teams were unbeaten; but Ohio State appeared unstoppable after rolling over Kentucky, Northwestern and Indiana, and cementing coach Francis "Close the Gates of Mercy" Schmidt's reputation for running up the score with an 85-7 smackdown of Drake.

Just a few weeks before the game, Ohio governor Martin Davey, already under fire for cutting the university's budget, provoked the Buckeye fans in his constituency – which was just about everybody — by revealing that 13 of Schmidt's players were on the state payroll, listed as employees of the state highway department, the motor vehicle department, or the state legislature.

"Football," the governor asserted, seconding a complaint more often heard in faculty dining rooms back East, "has become the supreme purpose of higher education."

But if that was the case, nobody in Columbus that first Saturday in November seemed to mind.

Once in town the day before the game, Layden tried to insulate his team from the hoopla downtown, where football pilgrims without rooms were camped in hotel lobbies and sleeping on pool tables. He bussed his players to St. Charles Borromeo, a secluded seminary in the Columbus suburbs, for a Friday practice that wasn't as private as the coach might've hoped. The Irish were greeted by thousands of Ohio State fans, some of them chanting "Catholics go home!"

On game day, more than 81,000 ticketholders wedged into Ohio Stadium, a giant horseshoe built to hold 70,000. Millions followed the game on the radio. All the big radio networks – CBS, the Blue Network of the National Broadcasting System, and the Mutual Network, with Red Barber doing the play-by-play — carried the game, the equivalent of CBS, NBC, ABC and ESPN televising the same Super Bowl. A small army of telegraph linemen worked through the night, stringing extra wires to the press box, where 54 teletype operators would be transmitting stories from the cream of the nation's sportswriters. Nobody could remember a more widely anticipated game.

At Notre Dame, Bill Shakespeare had evolved from a lethal punter who could run a little and throw a little – some of his punting records would stand into the next century – into a true triple-threat tailback. A two-time All American who led the Irish in rushing, passing, and scoring, he would wind up third in the voting for the first Heisman Trophy, behind the University of Chicago's Jay Berwanger and Army's Monk Meyer.

But when the Irish needed a spark after going into halftime trailing Ohio State 13-0, they got it from Shakespeare's back-up, Andy Pilney, a Chicago schoolboy star who'd been relegated to the bench for most of his college career because of his own propensity for fumbling, and Layden's desire to keep Shakespeare's powerful leg in the lineup.

Against Ohio State, Pilney squeezed three years of promise into one 15-minute window of genius, throwing for one fourth-quarter touchdown and setting up another, as the Irish closed to within 13-12.

In the final minute, Notre Dame got the ball back again. Pilney scrambled deep into Ohio State territory, where he crumpled to the ground under a hard hit, his left knee ruined beyond repair, his football career over in that instant.

He'd never play again.

While Pilney was carried off on a stretcher, Shakespeare rejoined the Notre Dame backfield. By now everybody in America knew the Irish were going to throw, and Shakespeare's first pass was almost picked off by Ohio State's Dick Beltz.

"If he holds onto that one," Shakespeare said, "we're all bums."

But Beltz couldn't hold it, and on the next play Shakespeare took a lateral from Tony Mazziotti, drifted away from the Buckeye rush, and found Wayne Millner in the middle of the end zone, to give the Irish an improbable 18-15 victory.

When the final gun sounded, Notre Dame fans poured from the stands, ignoring stadium security guards with nightsticks, and ripped the goalposts from their concrete footings, while Red Barber struggled to identify the pass receiver for his radio audience. His Notre Dame spotter had abandoned him, rushing to join the celebration.

A few hundred miles away, another young radio broadcaster working the Indiana-Iowa game saw the Notre Dame-Ohio State score come over the teletype, and refused to believe it.

"I couldn't believe Notre Dame would've been able to score three touchdowns in so little time," Ronald Reagan remembered in a White House conversation decades later, when he was President of the United States.

"So I never announced the final score."

Hours later, Hal Squier was in the lobby of the Deshler-Wallick Hotel when the Notre Dame band marched in, carrying pieces of the goalposts.

"If I never see another football game," he wrote in the next day's paper, "it will be OK."

A few weeks later, he was among the 75,000 fans who filled Yankee Stadium for the Notre Dame-Army game, a spectacle that had long since outgrown the facilities at West Point, where the game began as an afterthought to the Saturday morning parade of cadets, and nobody thought to charge admission. The family of Joe Sullivan, the dead Notre Dame captain-elect, was at the Stadium; his brothers sat on the Irish bench. In a locker room already bordering on emotional overload, Layden upped the ante, naming Sullivan's friend Bill Shakespeare the game captain.

This time the underdog Cadets, led by Monk Meyer, a pint-sized tailback who would wind up an Army general, outplayed Notre Dame for 57 minutes, before Shakespeare helped engineer an 84-yard scoring drive that earned the Irish a 6-6 tie, affirming their status as a comeback team for the ages.

Then he took the ferry home to Staten Island, the way Bobby Thomson would a few years later, at the end of another big day for sports in New York.

The borough president, Joseph Palma, met him at the head of a 200-car motorcade, accompanied by five marching bands, and they paraded through the streets, all the way to the Shakespeare home in Westerleigh. That night, more than 2,000 Staten Islanders crowded into a dinner-dance at Cromwell Center, a shipping pier converted into a quarter-mile long recreation center, to toast the neighborhood kid who won the game the nation's sportswriters, in balloting 30 years later, would call the Greatest College Football Game Ever Played.

And a few weeks after *that*, Squier was back at Yankee Stadium to watch Sal Somma and Andy Barberi play for NYU in the annual Battle of the Bronx.

Somma, a college junior in the fall of 1935, was finishing his second season as NYU's blocking back, linebacker, and part-time place-kicker, after a year getting his academics in order in prep school, and another on the Violet freshman team, in an era when freshmen weren't eligible for varsity sports. He hardly ever touched the football. Most of his Saturdays were spent blocking for tailback Ed Smith, the model for sculptor Frank Eliscu's original rendering of the Heisman Trophy, who first struck the stiff-arm pose mimicked by generations of Heisman wannabes.

Barberi, two years behind Somma in high school, was a year behind him at NYU, along with two more former Curtis players, Charlie O'Connell and George Blomquist. In Somma's absence, Barberi had blossomed into a wide-as-he-was-tall force of nature who could dominate a game from either side of the ball, part of *Liberty* magazine's first high school All-American team, and one of the stars of NYU's undefeated 1934 freshman team.

When veteran guard Ed Morsehauser was hospitalized with pneumonia before the next-to-last game of the 1935 season, Barberi joined Somma in the starting lineup.

The Violets went into their Thanksgiving Day tussle with Fordham undefeated, having outscored their first seven opponents 206-26, and daring to dream of a Rose Bowl invitation despite a downgraded schedule.

Against the Rams, they were over-matched from the start. Fordham quarterback Andy Palau intercepted two of Smith's passes and caught a touchdown pass himself, and the Rams won everything but the second-quarter bench-clearing brawl, in front of a crowd of 66,000.

When it was over, *New York American* columnist Damon Runyon, making a rare daylight excursion away from his customary Broadway beat, poked fun at NYU's weak schedule in one of his signature mock-telegram leads, addressed to the Rose Bowl committee.

"Dear Gents: Sorry will be unable to meet you in Rose Bowl (stop) We used everything against Fordham including our dukes but were de-emphasized again (stop) They have tough chins (stop) Suggest worthy opponent for you would be Andrew Palau and any ten other fellows (stop) Love and kisses (stop)

"The Violets (stop)

"New York University."

Down on the field, Fordham coach Sleepy Jim Crowley, another of Rockne's old Four Horsemen, commiserated with NYU coach Dr. Mal Stevens, a Yale-trained orthopedic surgeon and Crowley's friendly sparring partner at the Metropolitan football writers' weekly luncheons.

"I'm sorry, Mal," Crowley said, because at a time like that, what else was there to say?

"That's all right, Jim," Stevens told Crowley. "Maybe I can do the same for you some day."

7
The Seven Blocks

The way Somma and Barberi processed, distilled, and ultimately relayed the hard lessons of football to another generation of high school players had everything to do with who they were, and what was inside them. But a lot of what they knew about how to put together a football team, and how to handle young men … or how not to do it … they learned from Al Fabbri in high school.

The rest they learned at NYU.

By the time Somma and Barberi got there, the university was tilting back from its infatuation with "big-time" football, which was supposed to have ended when administrators, faculty and students conspired to run coach Chick Meehan out of town. Or, more accurately, *across* town, because Meehan continued to coach at Manhattan College for another six seasons.

College coaching was a different sort of job in the days when trustees and administrators still allowed themselves the happy fantasy that the young men who filled the stadiums on Saturday afternoons were an extension of the student body, brought together by serendipity and a shared affinity for blocking, tackling, and knocking each other's teeth out. Kind of like the chess club or the debating team, only with more bloody lips and broken noses.

Recruiting was frowned upon, and even the Rocknes and Pop Warners were expected to train whoever showed up for practice, preparing the boys as best they could during the week and then staying out of the way on Saturdays, when coaches were restricted to giving rousing pre-game pep talks, and overseeing substitutions. Coaching from the sideline — or sending a substitute into the game with instructions for his teammates, which was pretty much the same thing as coaching from the sideline — was against the rules, punishable by a 15-yard penalty.

"The game is to be played by the players, using their own muscles and their own brains," the sainted Amos Alonzo Stagg wrote on behalf of the NCAA Rules Committee in the 1934 edition of *Intercollegiate Football,* which compared coaching from the bench to cheating in a card game.

"If an onlooker, having seen all the cards in a game of cards, undertook to tell one of the players what card to play, the other players would have just call to object."

Even under those constraints, Meehan was a charismatic program-maker in the Rockne mold, with a flair for the dramatic, and a winner everywhere he went. His only mistake at NYU may have been that he did his job too well.

With Meehan running the show, the Violets were a powerhouse in the 1920s, with players like Ken Strong, who followed Meehan from Syracuse to NYU; and they played a steady diet of home games against some of the best college teams in the country. But like many of their peers in academia, administrators at New York's largest university had mixed emotions about that success, and the growing popularity of a game that threatened to overshadow the mission of the university; an ambivalence that could be traced all the way back to NYU's first intercollegiate game against Stevens Institute of Technology in 1873.

The trustees and administrators at NYU wanted to win. They just didn't want to appear to want it too badly, divergent goals that sometimes seemed as far apart as NYU's downtown campus in Manhattan's Greenwich Village, where most undergraduates went to class, and the uptown campus at University Heights in the Bronx, a subway ride away, which housed most of the school's athletic facilities.

As far back as 1905, spurred by the death of a player in a game against Union College, and calls from President Theodore Roosevelt to do something about the violent nature of the game, NYU chancellor Henry McCracken was the one who convened a conference of colleges and universities to study whether the game could be reformed, or should be abolished altogether, a meeting that led to the formation of the National Collegiate Athletic Association.

Six years into Meehan's tenure, NYU was embarrassed by a Carnegie Foundation report that a majority of the school's scholarships were awarded to athletes. Worse yet, Meehan had a habit of pulling scholarships from injured players or those he thought were under-achieving, a practice guaranteed to bring him into conflict with the school's Faculty Board of Control, whose members were already uneasy with the idea of a coach who was paid more than tenured professors.

Emboldened by the increasingly public discontent of their elders, student editors at the *NYU Daily News* ran an editorial calling for Meehan's job.

"Mr. Meehan stands for 'big time' football with all its corollary evils," the *Daily News* editors wrote, citing recruiting, the subsidization of athletes stashed in prep school for seasoning, "and a general drafting of students to the University for the sole purpose of playing football."

Days later, Meehan resigned.

But for a "kept" athlete, Sal Somma hardly felt pampered. He had to go to prep school to find out he was poor.

At MacKenzie Prep in Westchester, where he was sent to prepare for the academic grind at NYU — because even with Meehan in charge of the football program, NYU was determined that no "tramp" athletes would be allowed to play without holding their own in the classroom — some of his classmates arrived by chauffeur-driven limousine.

Somma earned his keep by working in the kitchen six days a week, saving what little he could, and second-guessing himself when he blew 30 cents on a Sunday double feature at the movies in White Plains. For him, even basic necessities were a burden. When a classmate walked off with his toothpaste, he challenged the suspected culprit and they got into a fistfight, before a contrite Somma found out he had the wrong guy. He spent the next few weeks borrowing toothpaste from a teammate. "I think he's getting tired of it," he wrote in a letter to his sister Mary.

His letters home ricocheted from reassurance ... "everything in the kitchen is going swell" ... to pride ... "we beat West Point (Plebes); I got two doubles" ... to self-pity ... "I would have come home Saturday night but my shoes fell apart" ... sometimes all on the same page.

Always, during the worst of the Depression, there was uncertainty about the future.

"How is the situation at the B and O getting along? Boy it's plenty tough now but if Pop and John lose their jobs it will be much worse. I will just have to quit school and go to work."

Periodically, he translated some of those sentiments into Italian, as best he could remember it, in letters to his father, leaving out the most anxious parts.

"We did the best we could for him," Mary Koffer said. "But

we didn't have any money."

In the spring of 1933, the football player who was so particular about his appearance later in life, always among the best-dressed teachers in the lunchroom, pleaded for his sister to send along a favorite sweater ... but only if one of his brothers wasn't already wearing it.

Later in the same letter, at a time when students were required to wear jackets and ties to class, he wavered over whether to ask for help replacing his only suit:

"You know that spot in the knee of my pants that you sewed... well it has come apart and I really don't know what to do about a suit.

"I have a chance to get a brand new (almost) blue serge suit with 2 pair of pants for $15 from some fellow. I think I can get him down to $10, so if you can raise $10 someplace I would like to get it. But don't do it if you can't possibly spare it, as you know I can get along with anything. It is only that I hate to see such a bargain go to waste.

"I had to sneak out of the kitchen to write this letter and the chef is calling me, so I will have to close."

The next summer, when he realized he was responsible for basic fees at the NYU football team's pre-season camp at Lake Sebago, Somma was so desperate to scrape together the requisite $57.50 that he deputized Mary to cash out the remaining $6 from his savings book account, and instructed her on where to find the penny jar he'd hidden behind the bathroom plumbing. The pennies were the last of his cash reserves, a few dollars he'd hoped to save for "spending money" at NYU.

But on the practice field and in the locker room, Somma was surrounded by players from similar backgrounds, almost all of them products of the New York City public schools. Like him, they were the children of immigrants, serious about football, and about making the most of this chance for an education they could

never have afforded on their own, with little tolerance for schoolboy foolishness. At freshman orientation, where first-year students were required to wear orange ties and violet caps, a fac-
tion of the Class of 1937 drew the line at Ducking, the tradition
of upperclassmen dunking unsuspecting freshmen in a 19th-Cen-
tury horse trough facetiously dubbed "The Fountain of Knowl-
edge."

When some of the football players balled their fists, the upperclassmen decided Ducking was over-rated.

For two seasons following Chick Meehan's departure, basketball coach Howard Cann doubled as NYU's football coach,
with predictable results. Then the university hired Mal Stevens
away from Yale, where nobody cared if he beat Tennessee, Ne-
braska or Georgia, so long as his teams held their own against
Harvard and Princeton, the other members of the so-called Big
Three, snooty predecessor to the Ivy League.

With no more Ken Strongs on the roster at NYU, and none
on the way, Stevens installed what he called the Rockne-Warn-
er Combination, employing all the passing-game trickery developed by Knute Rockne and Pop Warner, the coach who turned
Jim Thorpe and a hodge-podge of displaced Indian boys at the
Carlisle Indian School into the scourge of collegiate football, with
an offense built on speed, timing, and deception.

On any given play, the NYU backs might step up onto the line
just before the ball was snapped, changing places with receivers
who dropped into the backfield. On the next play a single blocker might be positioned on the short side of an unbalanced line.
After a slow start as the players adapted to the new system, the
Violets razzle-dazzled their way to a 7-1 season in Stevens' second year at the helm, spoiled only by the Thanksgiving Day loss
to Fordham.

With Meehan gone, as Damon Runyon drolly noted in the
New York American, the school fathers had dialed back the foot-

ball schedule, replacing heavyweights like Tennessee and Georgia with Widener and City College, and did what they could to
discourage recruiting. While Notre Dame drew players from across
the country, and the Fordham roster was full of boys from New
England mill towns and the Pennsylvania coal country, NYU
learned to take stubborn pride in its "city squad" of homegrown
players. Because all but two players on the roster were from the
metropolitan area, game programs listed players' high schools ...
New Utrecht and James Madison and Curtis ... instead of their
hometowns.

But college football was only growing in popularity. With a
few notable exceptions ... the weekend of the Kentucky Derby,
or a heavyweight championship fight ... big-league baseball and
college football were the only sports that mattered at a time when
the NFL was still scuffling to gain a foothold in the big cities, and
what passed for "pro" basketball was five guys in a Buick, playing church halls and high school gyms on their way across the
country.

And New York was still the center of the sports universe.

The city had the big stadiums, and the big crowds, and it was
home to the national radio networks. More to the point, it was
where the great sportswriters lived and worked. In an era when
most Americans had never seen a Rose Bowl or a World Series
game with their own eyes, syndicated New York columnists like
Grantland Rice, Damon Runyon and Jimmy Cannon told the rest
of the country what to think about the games, and the people who
played them. The hometown teams, Fordham, NYU and Columbia, didn't have to worry about scheduling home-and-home
series. Everybody wanted to come to them.

Everyplace else was off-Broadway.

Human nature being what it is, the writers never suffered a
shortage of material. They were especially fond of Sleepy Jim
Crowley, the Fordham coach and another of Rockne's "Four

Horsemen," whose life read like one of Runyon's short stories.

Steered to Notre Dame by his high school coach — the same Curly Lambeau who would be remembered as the founder of the Green Bay Packers — Crowley was tossed out of school in the spring of his freshman year, after getting caught in a dormitory dice game. For the rest of the semester he holed up in Chicago, routing letters home through his roommate at Notre Dame, so they arrived in Green Bay with a South Bend postmark. When he returned to school for the summer session and made his expected appearance with the football team in the fall, his parents never knew he'd been away.

As a coach, Crowley was at least as good a storyteller as he was a tactician, and a consummate showman. But in the autumn of 1936 he didn't have to work at stirring up interest in the newest phenomenon on campus: the Fordham line.

Fordham publicist Tim Cohane was the first to dub the Rams' front seven — ends Leo Paquin and Johnny "Tarzan" Druze, tackles Ed Franco and Ed Babartzky, guards Nat Pierce and Vince Lombardi, and Hall of Fame center Alex Wojciechowicz — the "Seven Blocks of Granite," resurrecting a phrase used to describe an earlier Fordham front line, and sharing it with his friends in the press box. Even before the name took hold, the play of Wojciechowicz and his mates had moved Grantland Rice to verse:

"Once Carthage ruled an ancient coast, but where is Carthage now?

The Grecian Phalanx no more wears the olive bough,

And where are Persia's ruling hosts, that ruled all warring lands?

Their day is done, by sand and sun, but the Fordham wall still stands."

The "Seven Blocks" owe their enduring place in football lore to Lombardi, who willed his way to the top of the sports world 30 years later, as the coach of the Green Bay Packers. But at Fordham Lombardi was the smallest of the front seven, and by most accounts the least gifted. When NYU's Mal Stevens wanted to call attention to his own star lineman, Andy Barberi, he never mentioned Lombardi.

"Barberi's every bit as good as Franco," Stevens told reporters, comparing him to Fordham's other guard, a consensus All American.

Once again, the biggest game of the season for both teams was the one played on Thanksgiving.

This time it was Fordham who came into the last game unbeaten, and entertaining Rose Bowl hopes even after a scoreless tie with Pitt — which had already beaten Ohio State and Notre Dame, the principals in the previous season's "Game of the Century" — and a 7-7 deadlock with Georgia.

As the Rams emerged as the best unbeaten team in the East, the crowds at the Polo Grounds grew bigger each week, and "California, Here I Come!" emerged as a staple of the Fordham marching band. For weeks, the new motto on Fordham Road had been: "From Rose Hill to the Rose Bowl."

Fordham fans had good reason for such optimism. The Seven Blocks hadn't given up a touchdown on the ground all season. Already, according to the sportswriters, there were feelers from the University of Washington, the host team for the 1937 Rose Bowl, assessing Fordham's willingness to make a New Year's Day trip to the West Coast.

"I feel at home with this squad because they're big and I can't pronounce their names," Crowley told the Associated Press at the start of the season, having long ago mastered the art of self-effacing humor.

But when Jimmy Cannon of the *New York American* asked what he thought about his team, Crowley didn't play coy.

"The best I've ever seen," he told Cannon.

The NYU Violets, with three losses already in the books, didn't loom as much of a threat.

For them, the 1936 season had been an uphill climb right from the start.

Encouraged by the surprising success of its "city squad" the year before, NYU tacked an additional game onto the front end of the schedule. But instead of adding another Widener or Bates, they veered off the path to de-emphasis by signing on for a road game in Columbus, Ohio, where "Close the Gates of Mercy" Schmidt's Ohio State Buckeyes and their fans were still smarting from their last-gasp loss to Notre Dame the year before.

If the school fathers were trying to kill the psyche of their inexperienced team — Somma, shifted from blocking back to fullback at the start of the season, was the only veteran in the NYU backfield — they couldn't have done a better job.

On the first play of the new season, Ohio State's Mike Stelmach intercepted a pass and took it the other way for a touchdown, first blood in a 60-0 wipeout. In the aftermath, Stevens moved Somma back to blocking back to make room for George Savarese, the fastest man on the Violet roster. For his part, Barberi had played most of the game with a broken arm.

Two weeks later, NYU lost again, this time to North Carolina, when Somma missed an extra point.

Even City College, usually a soft spot on the schedule, gave the Violets a tough time. Anticipating a repeat of the previous year's 45-0 walkover — a romp so one-sided that even Somma got in the end zone, scoring his first and only college touchdown — Mal Stevens left the game in the hands of his assistant coaches, and went across the river to the Polo Grounds, to watch Fordham play Georgia.

When reporters told him the first-quarter score back at Yankee Stadium was 7-0, Stevens looked surprised.

"Seven-nothing, huh?" he said. "Whew ... I thought we'd have more by now."

"What do you mean *more?*" one of the writers blurted. "City's got the seven."

Stevens hustled back to the Stadium in time to see the Violets rally for a 25-7 victory, vowing never to take another opponent for granted.

For the 4-3-1 Violets, the Battle of the Bronx would be their bowl game.

Somma spent the days before the big game watching practice from the sideline, his arm in a sling to protect a broken collarbone.

The night before the game, when the Violets retired to the New York Athletic Club's retreat on Long Island Sound after the obligatory bonfire and pep rally, he had trouble getting comfortable enough to sleep.

For the first time in three years, he wasn't listed in the starting lineup.

At the height of the Depression, the Battle of the Bronx was a chance for New Yorkers to get away from their problems for a few hours on Thanksgiving. Weeks before the game, on Armistice Day, a contingent of NYU underclassmen kidnapped the Fordham mascot, Rameses VII, dyed him a galling shade of violet, and paraded him across campus. But the game itself was no laughing matter. Hard feelings lingered from the year before, when the game was interrupted by a brawl and Fordham short-circuited NYU's fragile Rose Bowl hopes.

NYU hadn't held up its end of the city rivalry since the days when Ken Strong was running over everybody. But on a day so raw it kept some fans home, the Violets were full of surprises against Fordham, right from the moment Howard Dunney caught the opening kickoff and punted the ball back over the heads of the onrushing Rams.

Midway through the first quarter, NYU drove to the shadow of the Fordham goal line. From there, fullback George

Savarese, the speedster who nudged Somma back to his block-ing back spot after the Ohio State debacle, twisted into the end zone with Lombardi on his back, denting the reputation of the impregnable Seven Blocks, and earning the nickname that would follow him the rest of his life: Stonecutter.

Then Somma, broken collarbone and all, kicked what turned out to be the winning point, while Barberi held off two Fordham rushers.

Fordham answered with a touchdown of its own, taking ad-vantage of a muffed punt. But the Rams' regular kicker, Andy Palau, was sidelined with a badly sprained ankle, and stand-in George McKnight missed the extra point.

On the strength of Somma's kick, the undermanned and over-looked Violets still led 7-6.

After that, everything else was details. Dunney's coffin-cor-ner punts kept the Rams pinned deep in their own end of the field. Under leaden skies, the game deteriorated into a defensive stale-mate punctuated by an occasional snow flurry, but no more scor-ing.

Barberi, long since restored to starting duty, was in the mid-dle of most of it. When films of the game were shown on the NYU campus a few days later, his number 16 was so prominent that shouts of "Get 'em, Barberi," rang out around the room. The on-screen Barberi seemed to hear, manhandling one or another of the Seven Blocks on nearly every play.

"This was unlike most upsets," Robert Kelly reported in the *Times*. "There was no fluke, no intercepted pass with a long run that turned the tide against the favored team.

"Using only 17 players over the course of the game, the Vi-olet carved out victory with its own hands."

It was, Kelly said, "as if the gods of football smiled on the inspired fight of the Violet and made that extra point count so heavily."

As the clock wound down on the football season in New York, the NYU undergrads serenaded their Bronx neighbors. "Where, oh where, has Fordham gone?" they sang.

"The people went crazy when it was over," Somma's sister, Mary Koffer, said.

"The police had to get them to leave."

For years, she kept a piece of one of the goalposts, turned into souvenirs by the victors.

This time, Runyon played it straight:

"The complete crash of Fordham's celebrated 'seven blocks of granite,' undermined by Georgia's assault last Saturday, is at this moment reverberating all over the Bronx.

"New York University's football team, on the wee end of 5-1 in the betting, completes the ruin of a once noble gridiron edifice with a 7 to 6 beating before a Turkey Day crowd of 35,000 shivering in Uncle Jake Ruppert's refrigerated stadium."

Not everybody was as politic.

"The Seven Blocks of Granite," one wag wrote, "turned into seven blocks of cheese."

Somma's name was in all the headlines, a fact not lost on Barberi, who would soon be elected NYU's captain for the following season. The biggest game of his life turned out to be one more time when a lineman did most of the heavy lifting and wound up pushed to the background, while a back got all the attention.

"All I did," Barberi told friends years later, "was play 60 minutes."

It was an offhand remark that wounded Somma, who kicked the winning point with a broken collarbone, and stayed in the game long enough to get two teeth knocked out. But when pressed to respond to Barberi's not-so-subtle dig, he stayed in character.

"Andy was a great player," he'd say whenever the subject came up. "And a good friend."

Seven months after the greatest upset in school history, graduation exercises for NYU's Class of 1937 were held at Ohio Field, familiar ground for the football players who spent their college years practicing on that same expanse of grass. And when the band played "The NYU March" as the graduates filed off to the rest of their lives, it's safe to say none was prouder to have a Bachelor of Science degree from the School of Education than the railroad man's son from West Virginia, who had to raid his own penny jar for laundry money before he could kick the point that beat the Seven Blocks.

It turns out that wasn't the only time the Fordham and NYU players got together that season. Unbeknownst to Fordham coach Sleepy Jim Crowley, several of his stars had been slipping away on Sundays to play semi-pro ball with the New Rochelle Bulldogs for a few dollars a week, using football aliases like so many others before them.

Years later, a few of the Fordham players wondered if the 1936 season might've ended differently if their teammates spent Sundays in the library, or at the movies, and went into the Thanksgiving Day game with fresh legs.

But if the Fordham stars were worn out or nicked up from all those extra games on the side, their NYU counterparts should've been just as tired.

Fifty years after he kicked the winning point at Yankee Stadium with a broken collarbone, on his way into the NYU Hall of Fame, Somma confessed that he and several of his Violet teammates played for the White Plains Bears, another semi-pro team in the same league as the Bulldogs, pocketing $25 a game when that was real money to a guy who worried about frittering away 30 cents on a movie. The two teams met just weeks before their more-publicized "Battle of the Bronx" on Thanksgiving Day.

Somma was sheepish about the extra-curricular activity, even if it wasn't the first time he'd used an alias. But there was no mistaking his satisfaction over how that Bears-Bulldogs game turned out.

"We beat 'em twice that year," he said.

8

Kings of Vermont

Sal Somma never planned to become a larger-than-life coaching legend at New Dorp High School, the new school with the funny name ... from the original Dutch, *Nieuw Dorp*, for New Town ... down there in the middle of Staten Island, halfway between St. George and Tottenville, where some of the paved roads turned to dirt, and the suburbs met the country.

It took a war to get him there.

The place-kicking hero of the Battle of the Bronx came home from NYU with a teaching degree and a new bride, the former Sue Manez, one of the original Arthur Murray Dancers, who taught her halfback husband to cha-cha and meringue, and helped smooth some of the rough edges Somma brought with him from the locker room, the B&O machine shop, and the Appalachian crossroads where he sat up through the night with a rifle on his lap, waiting for the bandits or the river to come for him and his family.

Viewed from a distance, the record book makes it look as if he inherited his first coaching job, going back to Curtis High School and taking over from Al Fabbri, his old coach, the way a favored son assumes control of the family business from a doting father.

But it wasn't that simple, the way life is hardly ever that simple.

When the White Warriors started practice in the Fall of 1938, Somma was listed as an assistant to Irv Mondshein, who'd been designated as Fabbri's successor. But when Mondshein left for another job at the start of the school year, Somma assumed the role of head coach the week before the opening game.

It wasn't a smooth transition. He was having a hard enough time as a substitute teacher, staying one lesson ahead of his students as he bounced from one subject area to another. When he was forced to cover an afternoon math class, his weakest subject, Somma sometimes sat in on a more experienced teacher's class before lunch, taking copious notes. In the afternoon he parroted everything back to his own students, including the other guy's jokes.

On the football field, with only four starters back from the previous year, the rookie coach and his players were all learning on the fly. Curtis lost four of its seven games that season, and tied the other three.

"I didn't know if we'd ever win a game," Somma said.

It would be 30 years before he had another losing season.

In his second season at Curtis, the Warriors won more than they lost. The next year they went undefeated, heralded as schoolboy champions of New York City by the half-dozen metropolitan newspapers that kept track of high school football, which was the only way anybody "won" anything in the years before the Public Schools Athletic League instituted a formal playoff system of its own.

The year after that, Somma's kids went undefeated again.

To be back at Curtis, sitting in Fabbri's seat, a figure of respect in the old neighborhood, was everything he'd ever wanted.

"I thought I'd be there forever," he said.

Then the Japanese bombed Pearl Harbor.

By the start of baseball season, Somma was one of six million Americans in uniform. The Navy gave him a commission, and put him to work doing what he knew best. He spent the next four years supervising physical training for an endless stream of officers and sailors at bases in Texas, New York, California and Oregon, restricted to stateside duty while Navy doctors tried to get a handle on the stomach ulcers that would follow him back to the civilian world, dooming him to a lifelong regimen of ice cream and antacids, and nibbling on soft-boiled eggs while everybody else in the room was digging into spicy Italian dinners.

Years later, when he was coaching at New Dorp, Somma regularly dispatched players or managers on covert missions to Marty's, the luncheonette on New Dorp Lane, a few blocks away, for his daily ration of ice cream. "Don't get caught," he'd tell them, raising a conspiratorial eyebrow to let them know they were all in this outlaw venture together. He ate vanilla and coffee ice cream by the half-pint, spooning it out of Marty's cardboard containers with tongue depressors he bought by the carton as part of the football training budget. When a new New Dorp High School was built after he'd retired, workers moving everything from the old building to the new one found boxes of leftover tongue depressors stored in a corner of the field house.

When he was finally cleared for sea duty in the summer of 1945 — "It looks like I'm in the real Navy now," he wrote home — Somma went back to Norfolk, Virginia, where he started his military career, for re-training as a gunnery officer, expecting to join the fighting in the Pacific.

Before he got there, the war was over.

But by the time he got home, still wearing the gold braid of a Lieutenant Commander, Andy Barberi had settled into his old job as the football coach at Curtis.

Just as he had in high school, Barberi flourished in Somma's absence at NYU, captaining the 1937 team that lost to Fordham on Thanksgiving Day, and butting heads with Hall of Famer Mel Hein in an exhibition game between the New York Giants and the Eastern College All Stars. Before the war, he played for the Long Island Indians of the American Professional Football League, and helped coach the linemen at McKee High School, the vocational school just around the corner from Curtis, where kids who had no hope of going to college learned to be printers, plumbers, or auto mechanics.

For most of his football life, Barberi had been one step behind his old teammate, or two steps behind. Either that, or he was stuck in Somma's shadow the way he was that afternoon at Yankee Stadium when Barberi kicked the stuffing out of the Seven Blocks of Granite in the greatest upset in NYU history, and Somma got all the headlines for kicking the winning extra point.

Now, for the first time … because he got home first from a wartime stint in the Army Air Corps … Barberi was the one out in front, and he'd be damned if he was going to step aside.

Not even for Sal Somma.

With the only job he'd ever wanted already spoken for, and no prospects in sight, Somma found his next job in a card game.

A small circle of Curtis coaches, ex-jocks, and their buddies played poker once a week. The game was hosted by Ralph DiStasio, the captain of Somma's 1941 mythical city championship team, who ran a neighborhood delicatessen, just up the street from the high school. DiStasio's classmate, Bobby Thomson, who would hit the most famous home run of them all a few years later, was back from the war like everybody else, living at home with his mother and playing minor-league baseball for the Jersey City Giants, just across the river. He sat in on the poker game when he could. Thomson's old coach, Harry O'Brien, who coached the baseball and basketball teams at Curtis for 30 years, was a regular.

O'Brien had a house in Vermont, all the way up in the northeast corner of the state, where he and his family spent their summers. Every winter he'd cram five or six of his basketball players into the family station wagon during the Christmas break and drive north to Burlington for a few early-season games, and it was on one of those trips that O'Brien heard about a Catholic high school in Rutland that was looking for an assistant football coach.

Somma arrived for his interview at Mount St. Joseph Academy wearing his Navy dress whites, and was hired on the spot. His wife had to break her contract with the Arthur Murray Dancers to follow him to Vermont.

The Mounties already had a football coach, Barry Brannon, who coached the basketball team in the winter, and had enjoyed middling success in football, even if he never managed to beat the Mounties' natural rival, Rutland High School, the public school across town. But right from the start, players like Roy Rotella found themselves gravitating toward the new guy.

"He just had a certain charisma about him," Rotella said.

"He had a way of making you want to work harder, and convincing you that you could do it. The other coach was a hard guy to get close to. I think he wanted to be a tough guy. Sal was just the opposite. He had a love for humanity, and a love for seeing kids compete, and be successful.

"When you did something right, you'd look over to the sideline, and see him smile.

"That was your reward.

"Everybody was crazy about the guy," Rotella said. "We couldn't have liked him any more if he was our father."

The Brannon-Somma coaching arrangement wasn't friction-free. Maybe it was unavoidable, given their personalities. Brannon thought pep talks were a waste of time, and he rarely spoke to his players except to announce a lineup change. Somma was always talking to them, and not just about football. He talked about school, about the way they interacted with their teachers, about the way they dressed. "He was the one who taught me how to tie a Windsor knot," Rotella said. "To this day, every time I put on a tie, I think of him."

Personalities aside, Somma wanted to change some things, to install the Single Wing offense he'd used at Curtis. Brannon was a T-formation coach all the way, but Somma was persistent, and he got his way. The Mounties put in the Single Wing.

And they started to win.

By the time they got to their big rivalry game against Rutland, the Mounties were 5-0. For the first time ever, there was talk of a state championship at the little Catholic school on Convent Avenue.

Winter came early to Vermont; Thanksgiving, when there might be a few feet of snow on the ground, was no time for football. The Rutland-Mount St. Joseph game, the traditional season finale in that corner of the state, was played on Armistice Day, the second week in November.

The morning of the big game, it rained on the veterans marching down Main Street, and the Armistice Day services for the war dead were held indoors, at the Paramount Theater. But a raucous crowd of 3,000 turned out to watch as Funzy Cioffi scored two touchdowns and the Mounties, without a player over 185 pounds, upset Rutland for the first time in 13 tries.

"A new king of Vermont football was crowned yesterday," the *Rutland Herald* declared. Within days, newspapers in Burlington and Montpelier, the state capital, chimed in, making it nearly unanimous.

The nuns at Mount St. Joseph's were so excited, they declared a school holiday.

Somma stayed in Rutland for another year. He coached the jayvee basketball team in the winter, and the baseball team in the spring. On the bus traveling home from away games, he'd lead sing-alongs as the players got ready for the school's Spring Chorus.

Then New Dorp principal Mary McGinnis called him home to Staten Island.

Mary Camper McGinnis was a hands-on, no-nonsense administrator with definite ideas about the role sports, and coaches, should play in the education of young men — there were no varsity sports for girls at New Dorp in the spring of 1948 — and she left no room for doubt about who was running the show.

If the jocks were always going to be at the top of the student hierarchy ... and there didn't appear to be much McGinnis could do about that ... then the least she could do was put role models like Somma and Ed Ghigliotti, a Notre Dame graduate who had been coaching both basketball and football at New Dorp, in place to set the proper tone.

But their alliance, which would evolve into mutual admiration, got off to a bumpy start.

Somma had only been at New Dorp for a few weeks in the spring of 1948 when he attended a staff meeting where one of the items on the agenda was the design of a new logo for the school's athletic teams.

" I was thinking ..." the old Curtis fullback began, "if we took the block 'C' ..."

McGinnis's glare stopped him in mid-sentence.

"You're at New Dorp now, Mr. Somma," she said.

A quarter-century later, when he took the New Dorp football team back to Rutland to play the Mount, Somma's old blocking back, Funzy Cioffi, was the Mount St. Joseph coach. The city was still reeling from the loss of the Rutland Railroad and the Howe

Scale Company, two of the biggest employers in the state. But when they announced plans to throw a post-game steak dinner for the visitors at the Elks Club, players from the '46 and '47 football teams came out of the woodwork.

"Oh, my God, everybody wanted to go," Cioffi said. "We had to limit it to players and parents.

"It seemed like Sal had a way of touching everyone he came in contact with."

"He left a little piece of himself in everyone he met."

Forty years after Somma spent those two abbreviated football seasons in Vermont, a junior high school teacher from Staten Island bought a house in ski country, not far from Rutland.

He was having breakfast in a diner one morning, when a truck driver sat down at the next stool, and they exchanged pleasantries over coffee.

"Where you from?" the truck driver asked, picking up an accent he was pretty sure wasn't from nearby Chittenden or Proctor, or from just down the road in Plymouth Union.

"Staten Island?" the teacher answered in that tentative way people have when they're not sure the other person's ever heard of the place.

Brooklyn, he'd learned, everybody knew.

Staten Island, not so much.

"Staten Island!" the trucker said, having suddenly lost interest in his coffee. "Do you know Sal Somma?"

9
Short, Choppy Steps

Right from the start, Somma had a way with kids; not just for taking the disparate talents and personalities in a locker room and blending them into a team, but for knowing what teenaged boys needed before they knew it themselves, and understanding what they needed from him.

His genius as a teacher, and a coach, even more than the inherent decency and earnestness that rubbed off on everybody around him, was his knack for making them want the same things for themselves that he wanted for them.

And then making them think it was their idea all along.

"He made it all seem so … important," Carl Hiby, an undersized lineman on Somma's first undefeated New Dorp team remembered.

All the rest of it — the work ethic, the attention to detail, the idea that there's a proper way to do something, and we're not going to walk away until we get it right; the ingrained toughness that comes from getting punched in the mouth and coming back for more; all those qualities the millionaires and generals and state legislators who played for him would call the blueprint for success later in life — was the natural by-product of that central premise that football was worth caring about.

Al Fabbri saved Sal's life that day in the kitchen on Simonson Avenue, when he convinced Anthony Somma to let his son quit his 27-cents-an-hour job and go back to school to play a boy's game, and opened the doors to another kind of life. Somma would do the same thing for another generation of kids, who in their own way were just as needy.

And if that meant he sometimes winked at regulations that got in the way …if he knew some of the out-of-district kids who transferred to New Dorp to learn Italian so they could talk to their dear sweet grandmothers were really there because they wanted to play football, or if his summer workouts ignored the sanctioned starting date for practice … what did the suits at Board of Ed headquarters know about throwing a lifeline to a kid who didn't have anything else to grab onto? What could they know about giving kids a reason to feel good about themselves, and permission to dream big? And if you weren't doing that much … if you weren't at least giving them every chance you could to be successful … why be there at all?

Sure, he wanted to win. As long as they were keeping score, he was going to try to beat the other guy. "The fun is in the winning," he'd tell Paul Milza, his loyal assistant for 22 years. But it was bigger than that. Winning gave him credibility. It gave him the power that only high school coaches seemed to have with teenaged boys, and successful coaches even more than the other kind; the kind of power all the good ones used, in one way or another, to send the messages and drive home the lessons that no English teacher or assistant principal ever could, even if they were willing to try.

But it was never about feeding his ego, or showing everybody how smart he was.

"It was never about him," Milza was saying on a mild summer day in the Vermont woods, where he and his wife retired to a cottage so far off the interstate that the road turned from asphalt to gravel, and then to dirt, and they spent their winters skiing and their summers hiking on the same mountains.

"In Sal's mind," Milza said, "He was always that kid from Rosebank, or that kid from West Virginia."

"He always felt lucky to be able to do what he was doing."

He did it with an antique offense, the same Single Wing he learned from Fabbri in high school, and refined over the years with the help of Single Wing holdouts like Princeton coach Charlie Caldwell, long after everybody else had switched to some form of the T-formation. And he did it without yelling or screaming or cursing on the sideline; without demeaning kids, or belittling them, or using an epithet stronger than "jughead," which was his favorite.

When he was a young teacher at New Dorp, John Pecoraro helped baseball coach Joe Clark film games for Somma, climbing scaffolds and fire ladders, scrambling over roofs and in and out of windows with a 16-millimeter camera. They were making their way down from a rooftop in Queens one frigid afternoon, hoping to find a place to get warm between halves, when they blundered into a corner of the home team's locker room, just as the coach was in the middle of an X-rated rant.

"I was an excitable guy," Pecoraro said. "I'm sure there were times when bad words came out of my mouth. But this was over-the-top. We just looked at each other, and got out of there as fast as we could. It was like … 'Geez, is this how other football coaches talk?'

"We were so used to being around Sal, we thought that's how they all acted."

"Even when he called you a jughead," Larry Ambrosino said, "it was in a tone that said '... but I still love you.' He always gave you something to hang onto. He didn't know how to be nasty or mean.

"I don't think he had it in him."

Even when Somma had to sit somebody down, everybody understood it was never personal. There was a mandate to do the right thing that was bigger than him, bigger than them, bigger than any game. Somma was just the instrument.

And for a long time, he did most of it alone.

He didn't have an offensive coordinator or a defensive co-ordinator, a tight ends coach or a strength-and-conditioning coach. Until Milza joined him fulltime, Somma coached the line and the backfield, offense and defense, subs and starters, and in his spare time he cut up the oranges he bought at Barresi's Market for the players to suck on at halftime, and picked up rocks from the practice field. Whatever help he got came from his student-managers, who were always among the brightest students at New Dorp — two of his 1959 managers, Carlton Box-hill and Henry Malarkey, went on to become doctors — and trainer Tex Dawson, who taped ankles, supervised calisthenics, and could be counted on to break the tension in the locker room with a mildly bawdy joke.

Dawson, a transplanted Oklahoman with an exotic resume — tugboat cook, trainer for the old Stapes, groundskeeper for John McGraw's New York Giants at the Polo Grounds — fol-lowed Somma from Curtis to Vermont and back again. To-gether, they built a six-man blocking sled out of two-by-eights with their own hands, the way Somma was building a football program at the red-brick school down there in the middle of the Island.

"Mister Som-mahs (Dawson always tacked an extra 's' onto the end of Sal's last name, for reasons known only to him) wants you boys to git out they-ah an' hit!" he'd tell the kids in a drawl so thick that Mary McGinnis, the New Dorp principal who was a stickler for decorum, could only guess how colorful his language really was.

"Is Mr. Dawson allowed to speak to the team?" she asked Somma in that formal way she had of addressing everybody; and he acknowledged that, yes, from time to time Tex did have something to say to the boys.

"How do they know what he's saying?" McGinnis wondered.

As the victories and the championship seasons piled up, Somma's coaching methods took on an almost mystical quality, so even the simplest instruction — "Jog down and come back," he'd tell the kids in the middle of practice — was attributed to some Zen-like sense of when the players needed time to clear their heads. It took years for Milza to screw up the courage to ask about "Jog down and come back." It turned out Somma just needed a few minutes to figure out what he was going to do next.

Even when he screwed up ... like the time he lost track of the downs, and ordered a quick-kick on second down, thinking it was third down ... nobody questioned it. "Everybody was in such awe of the guy," Joe Clark said, "we just assumed he knew what he was doing." But he was never too proud to acknowledge that there were people who were smarter than him, or to ask for help.

Early in his tenure at New Dorp, he wrote a letter introducing himself to Princeton coach Charlie Caldwell, college football's 1950 Coach of the Year, and a onetime teammate of Babe Ruth and Lou Gehrig. In his short stay with the Yankees, Caldwell beaned first baseman Wally Pipp in batting practice, a slip sometimes mistakenly cited as the source of the headache that sent Pipp to the bench, and kick-started Gehrig's epic consecutive-game streak.

Caldwell's introduction to what he called "the science of football" came when he was a Princeton undergraduate playing for Bill Roper, an old-school coach whose notion that football was 90 percent fight — "the team that won't be beaten can't be beaten" — was shredded over the course of one long, frustrating afternoon trying to defend against the fakes, spins, and deception of Knute Rockne's Four Horsemen.

"I wasn't even tired," Caldwell complained in his instructional book, Modern Single Wing Football.

"I don't believe I made a clean tackle all afternoon."

After praising Caldwell's book in his letter, and offering assurances that he had no thoughts of becoming a college rival — "and if your policy is not to answer letters of this type, I will understand" — Somma launched into page-upon-page of inside-football questions; even remembering, in the days before modern copy machines, to enclose blank playsheets for Caldwell's doodles.

As it turned out, Somma's letter was the start of a friendship built on mutual respect. Each spring, Somma and Milza would cross the bridge to New Jersey and drive an hour down Route 1 to Princeton, or to the Tigers' summer camp in Blairstown, N.J. They'd spend the day in front of a blackboard with Caldwell and his assistant Dick Colman, breaking for lunch at the Nassau Inn. Even New Dorp's green-and-gold uniforms — with the stripes on the sleeves and the socks — were designed with a nod to Princeton.

For a "city" kid from Brooklyn Tech or New Utrecht, everything about the New Dorp Centrals, from their quirky offense to the leather helmets Somma managed to preserve from season to season, reducing the strain on his meager football budget, must've seemed quaint and old-fashioned ... like relics left over from another time ... right up until the ball was snapped, and Vic Esposito or Marty Ryan put him on his back with a double-team block he never saw coming, and Fred Fugazzi stepped over him on his way through the hole.

Years later, when Funzy Cioffi, Somma's blocking back at Mount St. Joseph Academy, was coaching his alma mater, he and his assistant coaches were at a clinic in Elmsford, N.Y., where Caldwell was a featured speaker. The Princeton coach was in the middle of his lecture when they heard a door open and close in the back of the room.

"Gentlemen," Caldwell said, "I want you to meet the foremost expert in the country on Single Wing football."

And when they turned around, there was Somma.

The Single Wing, once the dominant offense in football, was nearly extinct by the 1950s, supplanted by the T-formation as coaches at every level of the game sought to imitate the success of Clark Shaughnessy at Stanford, and George Halas with the Chicago Bears. Andy Barberi was one of the last to make the switch in 1956, after suffering through a winless season the year before.

But the way Somma saw it, the Single Wing, with all its intricate timing, fakes, and delays, rewarded teamwork. The plays in the buck lateral and spin series, in particular, seemed to take forever to unfold, requiring an act of faith on the part of a ballcarrier who turned his back on the defense, dependent on his blockers to keep defenders from cutting him in half, while all sorts of trickery was in progress.

"It was almost like a life-or-death thing," Paul Barchitta said.

"It all came with the idea that in the Single Wing, if all eleven guys didn't do their job, the play would fall apart."

Barchitta, another of Somma's players who became a coach, got to New Dorp as a wannabe tough guy with a pack of cigarettes rolled up in the sleeve of his T-shirt. He didn't get to play for Somma until his senior year; just long enough to learn to revere him. "Everybody had to block," he said. "Even the wingback ... on our team, he weighed about 115 pounds ... had to block.

"It was as much an ethic as it was an offense."

Not coincidentally, the Single Wing gave New Dorp a leg up on all those teams that only saw it once a year, and could never adequately prepare for all the spins, reverses, and misdirection in one week of practice.

But if Somma had decided to run the Wing-T or the Wishbone ... or if he had called out the plays from the sideline, so both teams could hear ... it might not have mattered. Like his college adversary Vince Lombardi, who got his start as an assistant coach and physics teacher at St. Cecelia's High School in Englewood, N.J., he built a winning tradition atop a foundation of fundamentals, repetition, and a passion for the game that leaked down from the head coach. All that was missing in Somma was the all-consuming ambition and explosive temper that marked Lombardi's climb from St. Cecelia's to the top of the football mountain in Green Bay.

"He was a gentleman," Marty Ryan, Somma's first two-year captain, said, "... and a gentle man."

A gentleman. That was the first thing out of all their mouths, a word you don't hear much anymore in sports. Jay O'Donovan, a onetime New York City councilman from Staten Island, was a New Dorp linebacker in the 1960s, with the scars to show for it, where a broken facemask gouged into his cheek and forehead.

"He was such a fatherly figure," O'Donovan said. "To see him get so emotional before a game ... it just fueled you."

Nobody, least of all Somma himself, ever took him for a genius. More than a few of his high school players, exposed to his penchant for forgetting names, secretly wondered if he was getting old before his time. And he was hardly an innovator. Everything Somma did, he learned from somebody else. Or he learned how not to do it.

"I wasn't a great coach," he would insist deep into retirement. "But I worked at my job."

As long as he coached, he never forgot the day in high school when Al Fabbri, unhappy with how things were going near the end of a long, hot practice, whistled everybody together, and called for a manager to bring out the water bucket. He waited until they were all around him, expecting a water break; then he emptied the bucket into the dirt.

"Now get back to work."

Somma loved Fabbri, loved him like a second father, but telling the story made him cringe.

"I could never coach like that," he told Milza. "I have to coach them with respect."

It didn't mean he wasn't tough.

For years, once he and Sue were back on Staten Island, he supplemented his teacher's salary by moonlighting as a bouncer at the Lincoln Lounge and the Melody Club, places where a cool head and a strong back came in handy toward the end of the night; and by umpiring sandlot baseball and softball games.

It was at one of those games, back in his old neighborhood, that he made a controversial call that went against the Rosebank Cardinals. There were rumors of some hefty betting on the game, which might explain why the ensuing argument was so heated. But in Somma's mind, one of the Cardinal coaches crossed a line. Later that night, he went looking for his tomentor, who had a reputation as a scrapper in a neighborhood where that counted for something. He found him at a local hangout, surrounded by friends.

The fight didn't last long. It ended when the other guy went through a plate glass window.

Nobody else moved a muscle.

"He was always too much of a gentleman to talk about it," John Pecoraro said. Years afterward, Pecoraro, who grew up in

Rosebank and heard the story from too many people he trusted for it not to be true, would sometimes press Somma for the details.

"That was a long time ago, John," Somma would say, and steer the conversation to what a good guy the other fellow turned out to be, and what fast friends they'd become.

"Even in his fifties," Ambrosino said, "he'd get into a linebacker's stance and bull his neck ... that's what he used to say, 'Bull your neck!' ... and you could see his forearms bulging. He still looked like he could break you in half."

But he never did. He didn't have to demean a kid, or smack him in the helmet to make a point, because he had that knack the way only a few men ever do, of worming his way into kids' heads, almost despite himself, and never leaving. How else do you explain one of his guys reaching back for a piece of the gospel according to Somma — "Dig in and take short, choppy steps" — when he was about to have surgery to remove a brain tumor, the kind of operation where nobody could say for sure if he'd come out alive or dead, or someplace in between?

Forty years after Lou Formica heard those words uttered on the New Dorp practice field, he was being wheeled into the operating room at Manhattan's Sloan-Kettering Memorial Hospital, when he turned to a room full of family and friends.

"Here we go," Formica said, and he raised a finger in the air, like a man poised to make a point.

"Short, choppy steps," he said, reprising a phrase that would become his personal mantra in the battle against brain cancer.

Mostly, Somma did it by being himself.

He didn't jump into kids' lives, the way the best of a later generation of coaches would. He didn't hug them, or tell 'em he loved 'em, like the fictional coach in "Hoosiers." Like a lot of men of his generation, that kind of display would've made him uncomfortable. But there was something about the way he carried himself... his Sal-ness ... that made them determined not to disappoint him, the way they didn't want to disappoint their own fathers.

"You didn't get close to Sal," Barchitta said. "I don't think he was aloof. He was just a very modest man. But if he looked at you in the hallway, if he smiled at you ... he didn't even have to say hello ... he made your day."

"He didn't tell you how to act," Joe Tetley said. "He showed you.

"Like he was teaching us to play the way he lived," Tetley said.

By the start of the 1959 football season, Marty Ryan and Vic Esposito were in their fourth year of playing for Somma. They were on their way to practice one afternoon, both still brooding from the day before, when Somma made a passing reference to how disheartening it was that some individuals weren't willing to give the daily effort it was going to take for the team to be successful. After a few minutes, Esposito broke the silence.

"Boy, he was really getting on me yesterday," he said.

"What do you mean?"

Esposito mentioned the talk about guys not pulling their weight, certain it was aimed at him.

"No way," Ryan said. All along, he'd been convinced Somma was talking about *him*.

"He was like a rock ... consistent," Joe Avena said. "You couldn't help being influenced by it. He gave you such a high standard to strive for, you never even wanted to cheat, or skip practice.

"And if he said, 'It might be a good idea if you did good in school,' you wanted to do it."

Sometimes you didn't even have to play for him to get it. Tony Zingali, who grew up on the same street with Funzy Cioffi in Rutland, Vermont, and coached with Cioffi for what seemed like forever, was a high school freshman when Somma showed up at Mount St. Joseph Academy in his Navy whites in the fall of 1946. "I didn't play football my first two years because I had asthma real bad," Zingali told the *Rutland Herald* when he was getting ready to retire. "But I went to practice every night and I'd sit in the bleachers and watch, and listen to Sal Somma.

"I learned more from that man than I could've learned in a lifetime," Zingali was saying after 50 years on the job.

"In retrospect, he was just a man, doing what he loved to do," Tony Brandefine said. "But he was such a man of stature, he could command the attention and respect of 35 or 40 guys ... guys who were cut-ups, wise-asses, tough guys in the street ... without raising his voice.

"You knew what he was telling you to do was the right thing."

In the Summer of '59, when he was in the fifth grade, Brandefine would tag along with his uncle, who played in an evening softball league at New Dorp, where Somma ran the summer playground every August. Almost always, Brandefine found himself drawn to the other side of the field, where the football team was practicing.

Before he'd finished elementary school, he knew all Somma's favorite aphorisms by heart — "The hard way is the easy way!" ... "You have to play with reckless abandon!" ... "You win the games Monday through Friday; you just play them on Saturday!" — and he could pick the players out of a crowd, just by their body language.

"Dennis Tancredi had a funny way of running," he said, "almost like he was galloping.

"Marty Ryan's nose was always bleeding."

"Sal was there in his shorts, and those black shoes with the crepe soles. He'd call out the plays ... 'Buck 32 ... snake out!'

"If you did it right ... if everybody did it right, because if they didn't, he'd make you run it again ... he had a way of raising that one arm in the air. 'R-R-R-I-G-H-T!' he'd say ... and he'd shake his fist.

"It sent chills down your spine.

"When I was 8 or 9 years old, I knew I wanted to be part of that."

When the time came, ninth-graders from Brandefine's neighborhood were zoned to go to Curtis, the big school on the hill, where Somma played for Fabbri. Brandefine applied for a waiver to take Italian, which was only offered at New Dorp, the educational green card for generations of out-of-district kids who wanted to play football for Somma. He wound up a two-time captain, like Marty Ryan, part of a perfect season, and the first of five brothers who would play for New Dorp.

"Those years were probably the highlight of my life," he was saying decades later in his living room, just down the block from the church where he helped carry Somma's casket through the columns of high school players in their game jerseys.

"Not in my *football* life," Brandefine said, wanting to make certain his meaning was clear.

"In my *life*."

He was there the day Somma dressed down his all-city wingback in the biggest game of the season, for celebrating too strenuously after a touchdown. And he was there the day Somma, disgusted that the coach at the Catholic school up the street was going to use a quarterback already playing on a ruined knee, cautioned his guys not to do any more damage to the kid if they could help it. That night, Mike McGregor's father showed up at Brandefine's house, in tears, to thank him for not hurting his son. And Brandefine was the one, because he wore the captain's number one on his chest ... Somma's captains always wore number one ... who went to the sideline when New Dorp was clinging to a slim lead in the fourth quarter of that same game, to plead for an early parole for two players Somma had benched for being out the night before.

"We need those guys," Brandefine begged, hoping Somma could hear the urgency in his voice. "We're out of gas."

In a world where coaches were forever compromising the same principles they once imagined were written in stone, Somma could've had it all. He'd already made his point by benching the miscreants; now he had a chance to win the game, too. But that wasn't his way.

He held Bradefine's gaze for what seemed like a long time before he spoke.

"Get back out there, One," he said, in a tone so clipped and purposeful it made Brandefine feel foolish and selfish for having asked, and prouder than ever to be part of what Sal Somma had built … something bigger than any football game … all at the same time.

"It was Sal Somma," Brandefine said. "It just oozed out of him."

10
Too Many Nice Guys

In August of 1959, while Vince Lombardi, the new head coach of the Green Bay Packers, was trying to instill a sense of pride and purpose in his sad-sack team, New York mayor Robert Wagner joined a phalanx of public officials wielding chrome-plated shovels at the groundbreaking ceremonies for the bridge being billed as Staten Island's gateway to the future.

While a crowd of 3,000 sweltered through the first hours of a week-long heat wave, the First Army Band played patriotic tunes and politicians spouted platitudes on the parade ground at Fort Wadsworth, the military installation that had guarded the Staten Island side of the Narrows since pre-Revolutionary times.

Even as work on the world's longest suspension span began, the bill naming it for the Italian explorer Giovanni da Verrazano had yet to be signed into law, despite an enthusiastic public relations campaign by the Italian Historical Society of America.

Dissenters complained that the name lacked a sense of place, and would inevitably lead to fuzzy spelling and pronunciation problems.

Not everybody was so subtle. In the bars of Bay Ridge, they were already calling it "the Guinea Gangplank," the kind of slur the Sommas first heard in the West Virginia panhandle.

As the speeches droned on, a small plane invaded Fort Wadsworth's air space, trailing a banner: "Name it The Staten Island Bridge."

Spent from their ceremonial labors, the politicians retired to the air-conditioned Officers Club, where a 12-foot ice sculpture of the yet-to-be-built bridge melted while they sipped champagne provided by John La Corte, founder of the Italian Historical Society, who shrugged off concerns about the bridge's name. "How many people are able to spell 'Kosciusko?'" LaCorte sniffed, invoking the name of Thaddeus Kosciusko, a Revolutionary War hero memorialized with a bridge connecting the boroughs of Brooklyn and Queens.

A week later, without ceremony or fanfare, work began on the Brooklyn approaches to the bridge.

And the week after that, on the first day of September, the New Dorp football team, defending New York City champions by decree of all the big-city newspapers, officially started practice, the same way they started every season:

Picking up rocks.

Calling the patch of dirt behind the high school a field was a stretch, like calling the two lanes of blacktop down on Hylan Boulevard a raceway, even if there were always a few kids eager to see how fast their father's Ford or Chevy could go on the lonely stretch of road south of the high school, where you could sit for half-an-hour late at night, and not see a dozen cars go by.

There were no goalposts on the New Dorp practice field, no lines, and no grass worth talking about. What there was plenty of was rocks; so at the start of practice the players lined up fingertip-to-fingertip, already in full pads, and walked the length of the field, picking up the stones big enough to catch their eye, and throwing them off to the side.

"When you think about it," Danny Boylan said, "all we were doing was moving the rocks around."

After that, they ran.

And then they hit.

Somma's teams scrimmaged on Wednesdays, but they hit almost every day: one-on-one, two-on-one, tackling drills, and the infamous Bull in the Ring, where the group formed a circle around one player, firing out at him in turn, as their names or numbers were called.

"My daily concussion," Charlie Langere called it.

His players might've been surprised to learn how much Somma disliked the full-contact practices. "He was always afraid somebody was going to get hurt," Milza said. But the hitting served its purpose.

"It made you a battler," Bill Chambers said. "Compared to some of those practices, the games were sort of a breather."

Until Mary McGinnis lured Somma to New Dorp, the Centrals — the nickname came from the school's location, midway between the ferry and the Conference House on Staten Island's southern tip — didn't have any breathers. In the decade before he got there, the football team went through six coaches — one of them twice — and won an average of one game a year.

The situation looked so unpromising that even after Somma's undersized kids surprised everybody by going 4-3-1 in his first year — more games than New Dorp won in the five previous seasons combined — and upset Curtis in front of a Thanksgiving Day crowd of 6,000, his friends worried about his future.

"Don't stay here too long," one older coach told him. "They'll break your heart."

His friends didn't have to worry.

For the next 20 years, all Somma's teams did was win.

At any level of the coaching fraternity, there may be no better compliment than the one Florida A&M's Jake Gaither paid Alabama's Bear Bryant. "He could take his'n and beat your'n," Gaither said. "And he could take your'n and beat his'n."

We'll never know if it was true in Bryant's case, because he never coached at A&M, and he never invited Jake Gaither to take the reins of that other team over in Tuscaloosa.

But we know about Somma.

We know because in the years before and after World War Two, when there were only two high school football teams on Staten Island, and one game that mattered, he coached both places.

And wherever he coached, that team won.

When he was at Curtis before the War, Somma's teams won the first three Curtis-New Dorp games, each one a shutout.

And as soon as he got to New Dorp, which had never beaten Curtis, he turned the rivalry upside-down. By 1959, Somma's New Dorp teams had won nine straight Thanksgiving Day games, not counting the two seasons the schools didn't meet because of a strike by the city's public-school coaches.

That streak was in jeopardy in 1956, along with the chance for a perfect season and another mythical city championship, when Curtis kicked a late field goal to take a 10-7 lead. As the ball went through the uprights, Paul Milza, Somma's assistant, was surprised to hear him murmuring, "Good, good ..." as he paced the sideline.

Milza reminded him that they were losing.

"That's OK," Somma said. "We're going to go down and score now, and there won't be time for them to do anything."

Sure enough, the Centrals slugged their way down the field ... four, six, eight yards at a time, without once putting the ball in the air ... and punched in the winning touchdown, and the game ended before Curtis could answer, just the way he said it would happen. And who could ever doubt him after that?

"If he told us red was green," Ben Sarullo said, "we believed it."

It wasn't just Curtis, his old school coached by his high school and college teammate, Andy Barberi, that Somma made a habit of beating, although for a sizable number of Staten Islanders ... the ones whose view of sports, and life in general, was that if it didn't happen on that side of the bay, it didn't count ... that would've been enough.

Three times in his first decade at the red brick school down there in the middle of the forgotten borough, the big-city sportswriters anointed New Dorp mythical city champions. But the landscape was changing, the way a lot of things were changing as the 1950s drew to a close.

For the first time in a quarter-century, New York City's public schools had a formal championship structure, one that divided the Public Schools Athletic League into four divisions, leading to a playoff.

The format didn't make everybody happy. The new divisions, arranged geographically, lumped most of the best teams together, almost guaranteeing competitive imbalance. But the coaches were careful to leave time, the week after the city championship game, for the Thanksgiving Day rivalries that were the spiritual and financial lifeblood of the football programs at schools like Curtis and New Dorp.

Once again, through no design of their own, Somma and Barberi found themselves thrown together; at once allies and rivals, each one needing the other, just as they were that day when they beat Lombardi and the Seven Blocks.

"Over my dead body," Barberi would roar, whenever anybody raised the possibility of eliminating the Thanksgiving Day games; and that was usually the end of the discussion.

Somma would raise his eyebrows or roll his eyes, only a little embarrassed by Barberi's bombast, but secretly relieved that he was there to say it. And if he had any misgivings about his team being thrown into the toughest of the four divisions with perennial Brooklyn powerhouses like Lincoln, Brooklyn Tech and Thomas Jefferson, while Curtis landed in the more pedestrian "Queens-Staten Island" division, Somma didn't let on.

He was too busy tending to his own house.

"There are too many nice guys on this team," he told them when he thought they were going through the motions in a preseason scrimmage. A few days later, the Centrals took it out on the kids from Snyder, from across the river in Jersey City.

When one of the Jersey kids took a cheap shot at Pete Chiapperini, three of them — Barchitta, Chiapperini, and Lou Russo — went after him on the next play, inciting a brief fight, after which Somma felt obligated to reprimand them.

"We don't need any gangsters here," he told them.

Then, in a tone that let them know he wasn't totally displeased to see them stick up for a teammate, "... but remember, if a fight breaks out, never take off your helmet."

High school coaches, whose job was to coach whoever showed up, and regularly lost kids to graduation just about the time they were learning to play, or their bodies were maturing, were almost always in a rebuilding phase. "One coming, one going," Somma called it, the constant juggling to make sure he always had an underclassman getting ready to replace a departing senior. But the core of the '59 team was already in place.

Marty Ryan, Somma's captain, could do anything that needed to be done on a football field. Ryan and Vic Esposito, New Dorp's best lineman and the last high school player in New York City to play without a facemask, were four-year starters, and fullback Fred Fugazzi had started on both sides of the ball since his sophomore year.

"The Big Three," the student newspaper called them, and it fit. Around them, Somma had plenty of willing, blue-collar kids, the kind he'd fashioned into winners wherever he coached. But the chemistry of the '59 team was altered by the infusion of seniors like Artie Truscelli and Danny Boylan, natural athletes who managed to get themselves eligible after years of day-dreaming their way through high school. By the time the season got underway, two of the newcomers were in the starting backfield, and all five were getting regular playing time.

"Coming into the season," Barchitta said, "there were a lot of guys who thought they'd inherited positions.

"It didn't work out that way."

On another team, or in another time, there might've been resentment toward the new arrivals from kids who saw their own roles shrink, or from their parents.

But in the fall of 1959, parents hadn't gotten around to living vicariously through their kids, validating their parenting skills with *Proud Parent of Valley Middle School Honor Student* bumper stickers, or lobbying coaches on their kids' behalf. Men who worked 12 or 14-hour days to put food on the table had bigger worries. Nobody's father complained to Somma about playing time. And the rest of it got sorted out on the practice field, or in the games.

Out there on the field, once the hitting started, it didn't matter who your father was.

"Everybody got their chance," Billy Chambers said.

"If you hit hard enough in 'Bull in the Ring,' you might get to play quicker, but everybody got a chance. And the older guys kind of took you in. Sal made sure that leadership was in place.

"Basically, it all came from him."

They were tough kids playing a tough game. The high school rules hadn't been refined to eliminate head slaps, crack-back blocks, hands-to-the-face, or blocking below the waist, and the general attitude was that it was up to each player to protect himself. Marty Ryan came flying downfield one afternoon under a kick, launched himself into Jimmy Danielson, and snapped Danielson's leg like a twig.

And that was in practice.

"It was 'no holds barred,'" Charlie Romanolo said. "You had a job to do, and you found a way to get it done."

The New Dorp roster read like the trail of Irish and Italian immigrants through Ellis Island at the end of the 19th Century and the start of the 20th. Ryan and Boylan and Chambers and Curran. Avena and Esposito and Russo and Miceli and Panzica. A lot of them were first or second-generation Americans, not sure where they were going in life, a lot like the teen-aged dropout Al Fabbri rescued from the B&O railyards 30 years earlier.

They came from blue-collar neighborhoods like South Beach, Grant City, New Dorp Beach and Rosebank, where the guy behind the counter in the neighborhood delicatessen was just as likely to greet them in Italian as English. From homes where nobody had ever gone to college, much less graduated, and moving up in the world meant finding work at the Telephone Company or the Proctor & Gamble plant, or getting a civil service job as a cop or fireman or sanitationman; something where they'd never have to appear at a morning shape-up, waiting for some union hiring boss to decide if they worked that day or not. After 20 years they could collect a city pension, and not be stuck doing grunt work with arthritic hands or on ruined knees into middle age, the way so many of their fathers were.

Any one of them could've wound up on the docks; or, as the joke went in Rosebank, making book. Somma took them in, gave them a reason to believe in themselves, and in each other, and permission to dream big.

For impressionable kids like Barchitta, the wise guy who

showed up at New Dorp with a smart mouth and a pack of Luckies rolled up in the sleeve of his T-shirt, it didn't take long to figure out that the football players everybody looked up to were the ones on the honor roll and the usher squad, who wore jackets and ties on school assembly days. "You saw those guys," Barchitta said, "and you thought, 'That's what I want to be.'"

"You got religion."

It didn't mean they were all serious students like Bob Johnson or Lou Springer, who went on to Ivy League colleges, or soft-spoken Matt Cavallo, who went to the University of Detroit on an academic scholarship. Or Fred Rathke, who wound up at the Air Force Academy.

They weren't all choir boys, either.

On Senior Day, Barchitta was drinking in a car outside school with a couple of buddies when Agnes Johnson, who supervised the usher squad, walked by in a group of teachers. The next morning, he got a summons to Johnson's office.

Every New Dorp teacher had a student secretary; Marty Ryan was Johnson's.

"Martin, please leave the room," she told him when Barchitta walked in. "I'm about to curse."

As soon as they were alone, Barchitta launched into whatever explanation struck him as particularly persuasive at that moment.

Johnson cut him off with a raised hand.

"You, Mr. Barchitta," she told him, "could talk the nuts off a brass monkey."

Somma had his own ways of dealing with the knuckleheads.

He drilled them until they puked.

Lesson learned.

Pint-sized wingback Dennis Tancredi, another of the first-time players, was so intent on hustling back to the huddle after every play, even in practice, that he sometimes bumped into

Somma, who was standing alongside the huddle, waiting to call the next play.

His size made Tancredi a target for every testosterone-fueled prank in the locker room, where nobody was immune. Marty Ryan was the towel-snapping king of the room, right up until the day Bruce Liozzi, an undersized back-up lineman, caught him in the tenderest part of his anatomy.

"By the time he got up … and it took him awhile to get up … I think I was on the third floor of the building," Liozzi said.

Somebody was always stuffing Tancredi in a locker, or coating his jock strap with deep-heat balm and watching to see how long it took, once he started sweating, before he took off howling in the direction of the locker room. Or they'd drive down to Great Kills Park in Fred Fugazzi's '49 Dodge at the end of the school day, and leave him there before the start of practice. Tancredi would run all the way back to school, two full miles if it was a block, and sometimes he'd make it before the start of practice. And once the games started, he played with the ferocity of a guy 100 pounds bigger, and never took a backward step.

"He bled green and gold," Boylan said.

"If you wanted somebody in a foxhole with you, it was him."

Like some of the others, Tancredi came by his passion for football naturally. Tancredis had been playing for New Dorp since 1949, when Dennis' cousin Jim and the rest of Somma's "farmers" waxed all the big-city teams on the way to the school's first mythical city championship.

"Playing football for New Dorp," he told his friend Art Mazza years later, when they were reminiscing about jobs and careers, "was the last thing I did for love."

As usual, the '59 Centrals had their funky offense going for them. To teams that only saw it once a year, the single wing was like nothing they remembered, with a "quarterback" who called signals and did a lot of blocking, like another pulling guard, while most of the running and passing was done by the tailback and fullback, who stood side-by-side in what later generations would call shotgun formation, three or four yards behind the center.

More than anything else, they were a team: 54 guys ... 36 on game days, because it was a privilege to suit up, and not everybody made the trip ... who wanted the same thing wholeheartedly, and followed one voice.

"The most cohesive group of people I ever knew," Pete Chiapperini said, after serving half his life in the Marines and the New York City Police Department.

And they had Somma, the guy who kicked the winning point against Lombardi and the Seven Blocks with a broken collarbone, and called the Thanksgiving Day comeback against Curtis. In a game where confidence ... believing in what you were doing, and believing you were capable of getting it done ... was half the battle, just having him on the sideline was worth a couple of touchdowns before they got off the bus.

"He got guys to achieve goals that, in their minds, would've been unachievable," Bob Sambataro, who played at New Dorp a few years later, said.

"He had some great players. But he took average players and made them believe they were great."

"If we messed up," Barchitta said, "we felt like we let *him* down."

He wasn't a polished speaker. But when Somma started to talk in those anxious moments just before a game, they found themselves leaning in to hear.

"Gentlemen ...." he'd begin ... always "gentlemen," even on the days they disappointed him ... reminding them how hard they'd worked for this opportunity, this privilege , and what it would take to convert all that hard work into what they all wanted. "Take charge of your man right away," he'd say, and they could feel the old excitement building in him, even as it was rising inside them, until everybody in the room... student-managers, white-haired trainers, even the teachers clustered near the door ... felt it, too, and wished they could strap on a helmet and be part of it.

"He made you think about what you owed to yourself, to your team, your mother, your father, your girlfriend, your country, your God," Barchitta said.

"By the time he was done, you would've followed him anywhere.

"The first time he did it, I almost shit in my pants."

On the Saturdays when New Dorp won, which was almost all of them, the bus got noisier as they got closer to home. "Down the Lane!" they'd shout from the back, until Somma would tell the bus driver to take them down New Dorp Lane, the closest thing to Main Street on that part of the Island, with a drug store and a couple of clothing stores and luncheonettes, and not one but two movie theaters: the Lane, which got the first-run movies right after they left the stately St. George, and the old place across the street that everybody called "The Itch," because you couldn't sit there long without feeling something crawl up your leg.

By the time they made the turn onto the Lane, the New Dorp kids would have the windows open, and they'd be whooping and hollering and making a general nuisance of themselves, pretty much the way Somma and his teammates did that afternoon when the Fort Wadsworth Pelicans beat Al Fabbri's Heberton Cyclones, and the new kid from West Virginia caught the coach's eye.

And because New Dorp in the 1950s was like any other small town in America where folks took pride in their neighborhood team, people would stop what they were doing and come out of the candy stores and the shops, and whoop and holler right back at them.

Part II

11

The Captain

"Ryan!"

The team bus was quiet on the way to Brooklyn the last Saturday in September, 1959, for the season-opener against Lafayette, the way it was always quiet on the way to a game. This was serious business, not a class trip.

"Nobody said a word," Charlie Romanolo said. "Nobody told you to do it. You just knew that's how it was supposed to be.

"You got on and shut up."

Somma, who sat in the first seat on the right, immediately behind the doorwell, liked the bus trips to away games, which always involved a ferryboat ride. They gave him time for some last-minute counseling.

One at a time, he called players to the front of the bus, where the seat next to him was always kept open for just that purpose. Sometimes he had some nuanced bit of instruction to impart …"now remember, on 44 jump pass…" or a few words of caution or encouragement. Sometimes it took the form of a question: "Can you make that block?" Almost always, there was a sense of how each player's assignment fit into the larger plan, and the implicit message that his readiness to do his part might spell the difference between victory and defeat for all of them.

This was Somma at his earnest best. A few years earlier, on the way to a game in Queens, Ben Sarullo was the first player he called up. Years later, Sarullo would become a highly successful high school coach in his own right at the Catholic school around the corner, Monsignor Farrell. But in 1956 he was a 16-year-old tackle who brooded over each missed block, and took every word of perceived criticism to heart; an insecure kid who only wanted to hear his father say, "Hey, you did good," words the old man didn't have in him.

That day at the front of the bus, with what seemed like genuine regret, Somma gave him a scouting report on the other team's two gargantuan tackles, who outweighed Sarullo by nearly 100 pounds apiece. By the time he was finished, Somma had done everything but apologize for putting him in such a hopeless position.

"I'll tell you what," he said, sounding like a man who'd made his peace with the hand he'd been dealt. "Don't try to do too much. Just try to hold your ground.

"If you can do that, maybe we'll be OK."

A few hours later, an aroused Sarullo had driven both the big kids out of the game, and New Dorp was sitting on a comfortable lead. By the time the game was over, the Centrals needed a police escort out of the neighborhood; not that it was the first time that happened, or the last.

"I knocked the crap out of both of them," Sarullo said, a reminder that when it comes to motivating eager-to-please kids, sometimes less is more.

There was a protocol to the front-of-the-bus conferences. "A pecking order," Joe Avena called it, just like when the old trainer, Tex Dawson, and Tom O'Connor, a young teacher who joined the team as a jack-of-all-trades volunteer, taped ankles on game days. The captain always went first; then the other starters. By the time the bus ride was over, Somma had talked to everybody he thought might play a role in that day's game.

"It was an honor if he called you up," Avena said. "If he was talking to you, you knew it was important."

In the 34 years he was a high school coach, Somma's teams always had one captain, never co-captains or tri-captains; or, worst of all, acting captains for each game, which in his mind was like having no captain at all. As a player at NYU, he saw the football team split into factions, sometimes along religious lines, Jews and Catholics. That wasn't going to happen to any team of Somma's, and he was always working to put the right leadership — kids who would set the example he wanted — in place.

Years later, when they looked back, some of his players suspected Somma manipulated the election process, dropping subtle hints about where they should look when it came time to pick a captain, or nudging an underclassman into a leadership role.

"OK, Joe," he'd say, "why don't you take the team for a lap." Another one of those times when he made them want what he wanted for them, and made them think it was their idea.

"He'd plant the seed," Paul Milza said. "The kids knew. Most of the time, they came through." And almost always, when they looked back, they agreed the guy they wound up voting for, who turned out to be Somma's guy all along, was the right one for the job.

Nobody fit the part better than Marty Ryan, a couple of inches over six feet tall and 195 pounds of slab muscle topped by a dirty-blond crewcut, with a jaw that could've been carved out of the Cliffs of Moher in his parents' native Ireland.

Tom and Helen Ryan had 11 kids, 10 of them boys, one tougher than the next, and such good football players that Gus Semler, who owned the private picnic ground across the street from the Ryan house in Grant City, where all the neighborhood teams played, cut a hole in his own fence so they wouldn't have to take the long way around to the field.

Dennis Ryan, the oldest of the boys, and one of the best athletes in the neighborhood, was a priest; and until Joe came along, all the boys went to Catholic schools, where the clergy eschewed football and other foolishness.

"My mother was old Irish," Joe Ryan said. "She thought going to public school was almost a sin."

It took some time, but Joe wore her down, or won her over. Helen Ryan decided that playing football for a man like Sal Somma, who wore a coat and tie to the games and didn't curse, wouldn't turn her son into a thug or a heathen.

In his only season of high school football, Joe Ryan ran for 11 touchdowns in seven games, good enough to earn a scholarship to Villanova, where they still took football seriously in those days.

College freshmen were ineligible. But by the first game of his sophomore season Ryan was Villanova's starting fullback, while the other team's sophomore star — a Long Island schoolboy legend named Jim Brown — didn't get off the bench until the second quarter. Syracuse coach Ben Schwartzwalder had some firm ideas about rookies paying their dues; rules that applied to everybody, including the greatest player the game has ever seen.

When his college career was over, Ryan was drafted by the Chicago Bears and the United States Army, which pulled rank. He played Army ball at Fort Dix, N.J., slipping home on weekends to scout New Dorp opponents.

By the time he got to Chicago, the Bears had forgotten why they wanted him. Ryan spent a season on the Philadelphia Eagle taxi squad, centering for a sassy scout team quarterback named Sonny Jurgensen and backing up Chuck Bednarik, the last of the 60-minute men, who treated some of the rookies to dinner, and took them on the rides at Hershey Park. The Eagles cut him the next summer, just in time for him to catch on with the New York Titans, in the first hours of the American Football League.

Unlike those AFL franchises bankrolled by oil barons or hotel moguls, the team was owned by Harry Wismer, a former broadcaster and public-relations man who didn't have a lot of cash on hand, and didn't see why the Titans needed a training camp of their own. They moved from town to town all summer, practicing on high school fields between exhibition games.

Ryan caught up with the Titans in Texas, where they decided he was a defensive end.

"I never played there," he told assistant line coach John Dell Isola, who knew Ryan from their days in the Army.

"Don't worry about it," Dell Isola told him.

That was on a Wednesday. That weekend Ryan played his new position against Heisman Trophy winner Billy Cannon and the Houston Oilers, who were on their way to the first AFL championship.

Somehow the Titans went 7-7 that first season, with coach Sammy Baugh drawing plays in the dirt, and Joe Ryan, who'd shrunk to less than 200 pounds by the time the team came off the road, playing defensive end for the team that would become the New York Jets, in what passed for pro football. But it didn't feel like a career move. When the season was over, he went home to Staten Island to start a family, and went to work as a high school teacher and coach; showing kids, by his example, that it was possible to be hard-nosed and a gentleman at the same time, the way Somma showed him.

"I never had one of Wismer's checks bounce," he said. "But

when you got paid, you ran to the bank so you could get there before the other guy, just in case."

Joe's brother Marty, the seventh of the Ryan brothers and the second to play for New Dorp, grew up sharing a bed with one or another of his brothers.

The first time Somma called him up to the front of the bus he was a skinny 13-year-old high school freshman, thrust into the starting lineup when New Dorp's starting center's appendix burst. He'd been playing with the bigger kids his whole life, since the first day he followed his brother Jim across the street to Semler's Park. Somma told him not to worry, that everything would work out. He was ready to go back to his seat when Somma put out a hand to stop him.

"How old are you?"

"Thirteen."

"If anybody asks," Somma said, "tell 'em you're 14."

The coach wasn't the only one offering support. Before the kickoff, Joe Bossert, a senior lineman, nudged him.

"Let me know if anybody gives you a hard time," Bossert told him. "I'll get 'em."

Marty Ryan never felt like the most natural athlete in the room. But he was tough and smart; a slashing runner and a punishing blocker, whether it was on the line or at Somma's old blocking back position, the one they still called "quarterback" in the Single Wing.

Right from the start, he was always near the top of his class, on his way to winning the Staten Island Varsity Club award as the Island's top high school student-athlete; one of those rare jocks who didn't think it was corny for the captain of the football team to try for the lead in the school play.

Early on, Somma warned him against dumbing down to the misery-loves-company standards of teammates who were doing just enough to get by in school, or the ones who weren't doing

Sal Somma and 1959 captain Marty Ryan
(Sal Somma collection)

Sal, far left, and the Somma family in West Virginia, 1921
(Courtesy of Mary Koffer)

The famous Staten Island Ferry, the only route to Manhattan in 1959

The soda fountain at Marty's, where Somma sent
student couriers for ice cream
(Courtesy of Charlie Perrino)

A portion of the crowd at the first
Curtis-New Dorp game
(Sal Somma collection)

The bridge that would change everything on the quiet side of the bay

Curtis High School teammates Andy Barberi (45) and Somma (over Barberi's left shoulder) close on the ballcarrier at Ebbets Field in 1931 (*Sal Somma collection*)

Charlie O'Connell, George Blomquist, Somma, Barberi at NYU: The men who beat the Seven Blocks (*Sal Somma collection*)

Taking a victory lap: Thanksgiving, 1940
(*Sal Somma collection*)

The Navy man and his proud Pop
(*Courtesy of Mary Koffer*)

Andy Barberi, who had the only job Sal Somma ever wanted
(*Sal Somma collection*)

Four aces; Marty Ryan, Dennis Tancredi, Artie Truscelli, Fred Fugazzi
(*Sal Somma collection*)

Joe Avena, who asked "How was that?"
after every perfect snap
(*Sal Somma collection*)

Vic Esposito, the last high school player in New
York City to play without a facemask
(*Sal Somma collection*)

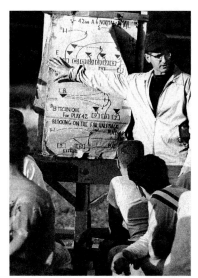

Clockwise:
Bill Chambers,
Charlie Romanolo,
Pete Chiapperini
(*Sal Somma collection*)

Paul Milza with the Single Wing playbook
(*Sal Somma collection*)

Danny Boylan being Danny Boylan in the
first official New York City championship game
(*Sal Somma collection*)

Marty Glickman and New Dorp High School
principal Mary Camper McGinnis on ABC's
"*High School Game of the Week*"
(*Sal Somma collection*)

Weissglass Stadium, Thanksgiving Day
(Courtesy of Charlie Perrino)

The last game: Marty Ryan drags defenders in the mud
(Sal Somma collection)

that much.

"You're going to do better in the classroom than most of the guys," Somma told him. "They'll expect that.

"If you don't," he said, "they'll lose respect for you."

By the middle of his sophomore season, still playing center, he was calling all the plays, a responsibility that routinely belonged to quarterbacks in the days before coaches started draining all the spontaneity out of the game by signaling plays from the sideline, or sending them in by runner ... or, in the pros, through a radio headset in the quarterback's helmet.

At 14, Somma was already putting him charge, as if he'd seen the leader Ryan would become.

"When I look back," Ryan said, "to let a sophomore call the plays like that ... it probably gave me confidence I might not have had."

When his teammates elected him captain before the 1958 season, the first time that honor went to a junior, nobody was surprised.

By the next year, it was a formality.

West Point wasn't the only college recruiting him to play football. But it was a big deal in the 1950s, when Americans still felt good about saving the world in World War Two, and patriotic Staten Islanders lined the sidewalks of Victory Boulevard for every Memorial Day Parade. It was heady stuff when 16-year-old Marty Ryan came out of church one Sunday morning and was greeted by John Murphy, a former Cadet First Captain and decorated combat veteran, who would soon begin serving nine terms as Staten Island's congressman.

"So," Murphy said, "I hear you might be interested in West Point."

When Ryan visited the Academy, the Army football team was one year removed from an undefeated season, and Pete Dawkins had just won the Heisman Trophy. All American Bob Anderson took Ryan to lunch. His parents were taken with the dark granite buildings rising above the Hudson, and the larger-than-life statuary of Eisenhower, Patton, and McArthur overlooking the parade ground ... the looming sense that this was a place where, as the instructors over at Thayer Hall liked to remind visitors, "the history we teach was made by the people we taught."

His timing could've been better. Ryan got to West Point the same year Roger Staubach got to Navy, which was like playing for the Knicks when the Bulls had Michael Jordan.

The Academy was still adjusting to life without Red Blaik, the Hall of Fame coach who guided Army teams through two wars, and coached three national championship teams, and Heisman winners Doc Blanchard, Glenn Davis and Dawkins.

And by the time the Class of 1964 tossed their hats in the air at graduation, the U.S. was hip deep in a jungle war in Southeast Asia.

"This is going to be tough," Ryan's father warned him before the start of Beast Barracks, the indoctrination period for new cadets. He lost 20 pounds that first summer; but the upperclass discipline, long road marches, and three-to-a-room intimacy didn't discourage a guy who played four years of football for Sal Somma, and grew up sharing a bed with one of his brothers. Ryan never felt pressured like his roommate, Brink Miller, whose father, grandfather, and brother were all West Point graduates.

"I knew if I came home and said it was too tough, it would be OK," he said.

"I just couldn't see myself having that conversation."

At West Point, football was the easiest part of his day. Blaik's successor, Dale Hall, who played in the same wartime backfield with Heisman winners Blanchard and Davis, Army's legendary Mr. Inside and Mr. Outside, moved Ryan to center on the first day of practice. He was Army's fastest lineman and best long-snapper, a residual benefit of his days as a single-wing center.

When Hall was fired after three straight years of losing to Navy, the new coach, Paul Dietzel, the first non-graduate to coach Army, shifted Ryan to guard. Four games into his junior year, playing on television against Penn State, he pulled to hit the end, future Green Bay Packer Dave Robinson, and was getting up to block the next defender when somebody kicked him behind the ear.

Once before, as a freshman, he'd suffered what the coaches called a stinger, and felt his left arm go numb. A pinched nerve, they called it, and Ryan took to wearing a foam collar as a precaution. This time he stayed down, on all fours, until the trainers came to get him.

"I was trying to get up," he said. "But the ground kept coming up and hitting me in the head."

X-Rays revealed a dislocated vertebra. There was talk of a spinal fusion, but the doctors at Walter Reed Army Medical Center were afraid surgery would aggravate the arthritis left over from his previous injuries.

His football career was over. Now Ryan faced separation from the Academy if he was deemed physically unfit for duty. He was pondering a future at Staten Island Community College when he went for his June physical, and found a sympathetic Army doctor who understood that once a cadet started classes in the fall of his senior year, he and the Army were committed, each to the other.

"Why don't you come see me again in September," he told Ryan.

That fall he helped coach the plebe team, but it took him awhile to make the adjustment from player to spectator. The first time the plebes scrimmaged, Ryan was standing behind the defense. When the offense broke the huddle and came to the line of scrimmage, he got down in a stance.

Two weeks after John Kennedy was assassinated in Dallas, Ryan watched from the stands as Staubach helped Navy beat Army for the fourth straight year.

"I remember wondering if I could've suited up, just to snap on punts," he said. "Maybe I could've made a difference."

With 20,000 American advisors already in Vietnam, and President Lyndon Johnson preparing to commit massive numbers of ground troops, the entire Class of 1964 was sent to airborne training and Ranger school; but the Army didn't know what to do with a new Second Lieutenant with a bum neck. Ryan wound up commanding a Nike anti-aircraft missile battery on Sandy Hook in New Jersey, a crooked arm of sand that juts into Raritan Bay, just across from Staten Island.

When he went for his next physical, the doctor looked at his records and asked about his neck.

"It's fine," Ryan said.

Just like that, he punched his own ticket to Vietnam.

He spent 18 months in-country, most of it as an advisor to South Vietnamese Rangers operating out of an old rubber plantation that had been used by the French as a school for non-commissioned officers. His counterpart, a Vietnamese major, had been fighting over the same terrain, first against the Japanese, then the French, then the Viet Cong, since 1942.

It was close, dirty work, in an area where the enemy owned the night.

One of the first Vietnamese phrases Ryan learned was "Nem ludan!"

Throw hand grenades!

On the darkest nights, when there was a new moon or heavy cloud cover, he'd put his men into defensive positions, cautioning them to hold their ground when the Viet Cong came for them.

"Stay here and don't move," he'd tell them. "Because I'm going to kill anything that comes the other way."

With so many officers rotating in and out, he became an old hand in that corner of the war. Majors found themselves reporting to him even though, as a 25-year-old captain, he was their junior in rank.

When the brass in their freshly starched fatigues visited from their air-conditioned offices in Saigon — always in the middle of the day, and sometimes with the rotors of their Huey still turning — Ryan would invite them to stay the night, just to see their reaction.

"The men would be honored to have you, sir."

Somehow, pressing business always seemed to pull them back to the capital by nightfall.

Talking around an unlit cigar, Ryan gave them the same primer he gave his 19-year-old radioman, drafted out of beautician school. "Do what I tell you, and I'll keep you alive."

Early on, he learned not to wear his class ring in combat.

"That way, if I got shot and had to pretend I was dead, I wouldn't yell if they cut my finger off to get the ring."

He volunteered to go to war, and volunteered to extend his tour. He went to Vietnam thinking the war was winnable and came home, just before the Tet offensive, thinking the good guys were winning.

"I didn't think we could be wrong," he said. "If the country asked me to do something, I did it."

It took putting some distance between himself and the fighting, seeing the same ground won and lost and won again, the whole thing going nowhere while more good men ... men he'd known and broken bread with, and learned to depend on ... were dying for no good reason, to give him a different perspective. "Some of the bravest people we had," he realized, "were the people who were against the war."

Once he came to the realization that he wasn't prepared to

go back, there was only one honorable course of action. Ryan resigned his commission. The Army responded by assigning him "outstanding officer" status, an administrative way of extending his service for another 18 months. Then he got out, went into the corporate world, and got semi-rich in the pension-consultant business.

Forty years later, with the Untied States embroiled in another ill-advised war, he remained disappointed in the leaders who should've known better, but no less proud to have served.

"I consider myself a wounded hawk," he was saying over lunch at the Gardiners Bay Country Club on Shelter Island. Out there between the South Fork and North Fork of Long Island, where new money mixes with old money, nobody seemed to mind that Marty Ryan made his the old-fashioned way, thanks to the lessons he learned at home, and on a rocky high school football field, and in places where a man was smart not to wear jewelry to a fight unless he was prepared to stay quiet while somebody cut off his finger.

A lot had changed since Captain Martin Ryan was trying to keep 19-year-olds alive in the jungles of Southeast Asia, and he didn't think America could be wrong. But when he watched the fresh-faced Cadets march onto the field before the start of an Army-Navy game, they didn't look much different than his classmates in the summer of 1960.

"You hear people say, 'I'd go to war with these guys,'" he said. "But at the academies, it's real.

"Who do you trust? Who can you depend on? That's always in these guys' minds. A lot of it's about commitment ... the commitment they make to each other, and to the country.

"It sounds hokey, but it's true."

And one other thing hadn't changed.

Decades after his playing days were over, Ryan was watching an Army-Navy game on television with his son, who was 12 at the time.

After the game, they had plans to go bowling.

The cycle of good years and bad had swung in Army's favor, and Navy didn't have any Staubachs or Joe Bellinos to shift the balance of power. When Army built a big lead in the third quarter, young Tim Ryan was ready to bolt.

"The game's not over," Marty said.

His son argued that anybody could see Army was going to win.

"You don't understand," Marty Ryan found himself saying, 30 years after wondering if he could've suited up with a couple of damaged vertebrae when Army played Navy.

"I don't just want to beat them," he told his son.

"I want to beat them so bad they make an announcement the next day that they're giving up the sport."

The New Dorp Centrals didn't need any heroics from their captain in the 1959 season opener against Lafayette, the first of the five Brooklyn schools on their schedule.

The night before the game, Ryan had a dream about the game, which hardly ever happened. In the dream, he remembered catching a pass and running for a touchdown.

Weird, he thought to himself, and forgot all about it.

The first day of the high school football season in New York was an Indian Summer Saturday. Back on Staten Island, Andy Barberi's Curtis Warriors opened the season with a one-sided loss to Flushing, which didn't surprise anybody who remembered the previous season, when the Warriors lost six out of seven games, and tied the seventh. But for the New Dorp kids, even the ferry ride to Brooklyn was as smooth as glass.

"Don't give the ball to Truscelli on the first play," Somma told Ryan in their time together on the bus. "But give it to him as soon as you can, before he has time to get nervous."

Somma didn't have to worry. The first time Artie Truscelli touched the ball in a high school football game, he lofted a perfect pass to Ryan, who caught it at the Lafayette 20-yard line. When he turned to take on the closest defender, there was nobody there.

Three plays into the first game, and already it was turning into a dream season.

Truscelli wasn't done. He threw two more touchdown passes to Charlie Romanolo and Bill Chambers, and the Centrals shut out Lafayette 22-0. When it was over, they gathered around Somma in the locker room, sweaty and dirty, bone-tired and full of themselves, remembering all over again how much fun it was when they won.

All that remained was the awarding of the game ball, which always went to the captain after the first victory of a new season.

Except this year.

This time, Somma told them, he'd decided to switch things up. The captain would get the game ball after the Curtis game on Thanksgiving, which would be more meaningful.

It was out of character for Somma to get ahead of himself like that; but he'd made a decision, and that was that. And besides, there were needier kids in that circle of eager faces, kids who needed the affirmation more than Marty Ryan, who already seemed destined for bigger things.

"And the game ball goes to …" Somma said, all their eyes on him, "… Fred Fugazzi."

12
Fred's World

Fred Fugazzi was trouble, anybody could see that.

Paul Milza saw it, right off.

If you searched the classrooms and hallways of the high school for a week, you couldn't have found two more polar opposites than Fugazzi, the babyfaced tough who went through life with a chip on his shoulder, ready to fight at the drop of a hat, and Milza, the soft-spoken assistant football coach who'd been in training for that job since the day he and his friend Charlie Kemether went to the first-ever Curtis-New Dorp game, when they were in the eighth grade.

Milza and Kemether got to the ballpark before the gates were open, and Milza fell in love with the game and everything about it.

He never got to play for Somma, who was still in the Navy when Milza was part of an 0-8 New Dorp team as a high school senior. A few years later, when he was home from college and his brother Ed was on the team, Milza went back to watch practice the night before the Thanksgiving Day game.

"We're getting ready to have a meeting," Somma told him. "Why don't you come down?"

A year earlier, in Somma's first season at New Dorp, the seniors asked if they could say a few words the night before the Curtis game, the start of a yearly ritual that would become as much a tradition as the game itself.

Every team has its natural leaders. Frank Walter, Somma's captain in 1949, would go on to become a full colonel in the Air Force. But it was Mike Dicenza, normally the quiet type, who surprised his teammates with a passionate plea for victory, reminding them how far they'd come to be on the cusp of an undefeated season, and how close they were to doing something they'd remember the rest of their lives.

"Are you going to let it get away?" he asked them.

These were tough kids, including a few Milza knew from the neighborhood, and he was struck by such an open display of emotion.

"Some of them were crying," he said.

After that, there was no place else he wanted to be.

Tall, thin, and bespectacled, Milza didn't look like anybody's picture of a football coach. And if Somma was a gentleman from the old school, Milza was even more deferential if that was possible, and so straight-laced he'd look at the floor, scuffing his feet in obvious discomfort, whenever Somma called on Tex Dawson to tell one of his colorful locker room stories.

The only time anybody could remember him using bad language ... when he let a whispered "Oh, shit!" slip out over a play gone awry in practice ... he felt the need to call the entire team together at the end of the day.

"Gentlemen," he told them as solemnly as if they were in church, "I owe you an apology.

"There's no excuse for me using that kind of language."

To Milza's way of thinking, some of Somma's best coaching was done when the kids were gathered around him on one knee, and the conversation was only tangentially connected to football. It was those times when Somma explained why the hard way really was the easy way ... "when you're still fresh in the fourth quarter and the guy across from you is wearing down, and you can see he's ready to quit, then you'll know why you did all that running in August and September" ... or why they should make eye contact and say hello when a teacher passed them in the hall.

"That teacher has something you want," he'd tell them.

And because he was Sal Somma, they listened.

"He built a real pride in them, and it showed in the way they practiced and the way they played," Milza said. "Those kids would've done anything for him."

And because Milza understood that the kids who were the quickest to rebel against the structure and discipline of a team game — the ones a coach might be tempted to get rid of first — were often the ones who needed it most, he saw something in the kid with the chip on his shoulder.

Mostly, he saw the need.

He wasn't the first. Fugazzi was a puzzle: a rebel from a solid family; a brawler who read voraciously and listened to opera, at once smart and stubborn and loyal to a fault, charismatic and more than a little dangerous; more worldly than any of his classmates but constitutionally incapable of walking away from a confrontation, or anything else, except on his own unyielding terms.

Despite all that, or maybe because of it, he drew people to him the way he drew trouble. Guys. Girls. Their mothers and fathers. "It was like a magnetic thing," Danny Boylan said.

"He just drew people in."

"Everybody knew Freddie," Paul Barchitta said. "What was

unbelievable was that he knew me."

And because he had so much to offer, and seemed always on the brink of throwing it away over some cause only he could see, there was always somebody trying to nudge him back from the abyss. Father Gordon, the parish priest at St. Ann's in New Dorp. Anthony Caporaso, the teacher at PS 48 who got him interested in books, and in being more than the toughest guy on the block. Milt Huttner, a caddy at the local country club, who wrote letters to colleges that played Single Wing football until he found a coach who took an interest in Fugazzi, and started a pipeline that funneled generations of New Dorp players to tiny Missouri Valley College, halfway across the country.

Milza started by pulling him into the gym at the end of the school day, engaging him in long conversations in the bleachers while the basketball team got ready for practice. That way, at least, Fugazzi wasn't part of the after-school crowd at the bus stop, where so much mischief started.

Some of the time, they talked about sports. Milza had seen enough in gym class to know Fugazzi was a natural athlete, but he hadn't signed up for anything as a freshman.

"Are you afraid of failing?" Milza asked during one of their conversations in the bleachers.

If Fugazzi hadn't already made up his mind to play football, that challenge sealed the deal.

On the football field, where premeditated violence was part of the game, he played with a near-perfect blend of power, speed and aggression. He was a punishing fullback and linebacker, good enough to score 39 college touchdowns at Missouri Valley, where coach Volney Ashford, a straight-as-an-arrow Baptist who didn't drink or smoke or raise hell with referees, did his best to look the other way when word of Fugazzi's indiscretions reached campus. Good enough to be drafted by the Boston Patriots of the American Football League.

If he didn't already have a ruined shoulder from playing ball in the Marines by the time he got to a pro camp, Fugazzi might've wound up playing on Sundays.

One thing was certain; nobody was going to tell him he couldn't.

"He had a tremendous amount of pride in himself," Milza said. "And he wanted to do well in football so badly. When he was a sophomore and we ran Buck 36 or Buck 38 ... one of those plays where the fullback goes up the middle ... he'd try to run over the linebackers.

"By the time he was a senior, he learned to make them miss."

It didn't hurt that he had that meanness about him.

"Remember," he told Barchitta after leveling him with a fore-arm during a Friday workout without helmets, "it's a jungle out here."

Just once, Fugazzi lost his temper in a game, when one of the Far Rockaway kids was gouging his face at the bottom of a pile. "He kicked the guy, hoping he'd fight," Marty Ryan said. "The problem was he kicked the wrong guy."

The officials saw it, and threw him out of the game. That was another time the Centrals needed a police escort out of the neighborhood, all the way to the 69th Street Ferry. Somma kept Fugazzi on the bench the next week, even though he didn't have to, and after that he learned to keep his composure, the way he learned it was easier to go around the linebackers instead of trying to run through them.

"He was the personification of what football was about," Danny Boylan said. "He never backed down. He never took the easy way out.

"He'd come back to the huddle ... and he probably just got six, seven, eight yards all by himself ... and he'd say, 'Geez, that was a great block.'"

Off the field was a whole other story.

Avena, who was his teammate for three years in high school and four more in college, and his friend long after that, guessed Fugazzi was in a hundred fights in the time they knew each other. And those were just the ones he knew about, because Fugazzi never talked about his battles, the way he never talked about the women; and there were a few of them, too.

He wasn't a classic bully, the kind who got his kicks pushing little guys around.

"If some big guy was giving you a hard time, he was the first one to come to your rescue," Artie Truscelli said.

"Like Sir Lancelot," he said.

"It was like he had his own code," Marty Ryan said, and that was a phrase a lot of them used when they talked about Fugazzi. "I never saw him pick on anybody smaller than him."

A lot of the fights were bar fights. The drinking age in New York was 18, but in the '50s bartenders weren't always fussy about checking proof; a kid like Fugazzi, who always looked and acted older, never had any problem getting served. But it wasn't beer muscles that got him in trouble. He'd see some wannabe tough guy bullying somebody he knew, or somebody he didn't, or hear some loudmouth making a scene on the other side of the room, and he'd have to put the guy in his place, right then and there, the only way he knew. And if the other guy wasn't big enough or tough enough to make it a fair fight, he'd wait to see if the guy had a friend who met his standards. Then he'd confront the guy he'd decided he didn't like.

"Is that big guy your friend?"

The other guy would say, yeah, he was.

"Good," Fugazzi would tell him. "Because that's the guy I'm gonna beat the crap out of."

He didn't win them all. But he never lost, because to stop him you would've had to beat him until he was unconscious, or dead, and there weren't a lot of guys ready to go that far; and the odds never bothered him. Four-against-one, five-against one, a bar full of bikers … it didn't matter, once he'd made up his mind. When they were in college, he and Avena were the only white guys in a Missouri roadhouse when Fugazzi got into a scrap with a guy, and followed him out to his car. When he tried to drive away, Fugazzi grabbed the door handle, and the other guy pulled a gun from under the seat and took a shot at him.

Somehow, even at that close range, the shot missed, maybe because the shooter was so scared. But it wasn't the first time somebody pulled a gun on Fugazzi; and it wouldn't be the last.

"Sometimes," Avena said, "I think he wanted to die."

A lot of times, unless the other guy was a total jerk, he'd feel bad afterward, and want to make things right. Then he'd wind up apologizing, even if it was the next day or the next week or a year later, and more often than not the two of them would shake hands and wind up friends. And that was the other thing about Fugazzi; if you were his friend, you were his friend for life.

"If he saw good in a person … and it could've been the same guy he beat up the week before … he'd find a way to do the right thing for somebody who needed help," Avena said.

"A lot of the time it came from him knowing, without the other person asking.

"You didn't have to ask," Avena said.

More than most people, Avena got to see another side of the tough guy who liked to lay teammates out in practice, just to see if they were paying attention. After college, he and Fugazzi worked as counselors at Mount Loretto, the largest orphanage and foster care facility east of the Mississippi, down there on Staten Island's rural South Shore, where cows grazed by the side of the road, and the Mount's open fields ran for half-a-mile to the water's edge.

For the boys, sports were the lifeblood of the Mount. Fugazzi would pull up the lane in his red Spitfire convertible, and the kids would come running.

"We gonna play football today?"

Fugazzi gave them the smile that only his friends got to see. "Does a bear shit in the woods?"

After the Marines, and after the fling with the Patriots didn't work out, he became a fireman, and for one memorable season he and Avena coached a Pop Warner team at the Mount. Fugazzi, always the outlaw, coached the defense, and in practice sometimes he'd tell his defenders to jump offside before the snap, giving them a free shot at the kids on the other side of the line.

"That usually set the tone for practice," Avena said. "I'd get pissed off at Fred, but nobody ever got hurt and the defense loved it, and they loved Fred for letting them do it.

"He was great with kids, especially the kids with problems. I don't know if he saw something of himself ... but the wilder, the tougher, the nastier they were, the more he reached out to them.

"He was always a guy for the underdog."

Even so, being his friend could be draining.

Years later, when they were old married folks in their 30s, Avena and his wife stopped in a tavern to have a beer with Fugazzi. Linda Avena made a detour to the ladies' room while they waited for their drinks, and she was on her way back to her seat when Joe took her by the arm.

"C'mon," he said, steering her toward the door, "we've got to go."

Somehow, Fugazzi managed to get in a fight — and finish it — in the few minutes she was gone, and somebody had called the cops.

There were a dozen stories like that. Two dozen. "Going out with him was kind of like being with a gunslinger in the Old West," Avena said. "You'd go into a place and there'd be three or four guys there, waiting to challenge him. You were always on edge, looking around, wondering when it was going to start. By the time you walked out, you were exhausted, even if nothing happened."

Nobody who knew him was surprised when Fugazzi won the Fire Department's highest honor for pulling two men from a burning building. Mayor John Lindsay handed him the medal. A few years later, he went into the East River in the middle of winter to rescue two women after their car veered off the FDR Drive, and into the water.

"I guess he was a good fireman," Avena said. "He probably went farther than he should've, but it wasn't because he was a fireman. He never talked like that, the way some guys do.

"It was the way he did things," Avena said.

But it was never enough, the way football was never enough.

They were in the city one night when Avena blurted out something that had been bouncing around in his head for awhile.

"If you keep going like this," he told Fugazzi, "you'll never make it to 40."

As it turned out, he didn't make it to 37.

For once, he wasn't the one who started the fight, which began as an argument over the pool table in a place called the Fremont Lounge. Fugazzi saw one of the pool players, who was really just a kid, was getting the worst of it, so he stepped in to break up the fight, and pushed the other guy into the kitchen; one more time when he was the one sticking up for the underdog. Only this time the other guy pulled out a gun when Fugazzi followed him into the kitchen, and shot him dead. He was 36, and a full-grown legend in the old neighborhood.

"He was the Fonz," somebody was saying years later when a bunch of the old New Dorp guys were having lunch, meaning the leather-jacketed ladies' man played by Henry Winkler in the '70s television show "Happy Days."

Paul Barchitta snorted.

"You got it backwards," Barchitta said. "The Fonz was Freddie."

When somebody repeated that line to Marty Ryan, he nodded. When they were still in high school, and he heard Fugazzi was out the night before a game, and in another fight, Ryan confronted him. The captain, who didn't drink and never went anywhere the night before a game, told Fugazzi he shouldn't be drinking, and he sure shouldn't be getting into any fights the night before a football game. If he got himself benched, Ryan told him, he'd be letting the whole team down.

Fugazzi took the dressing down the way he didn't take much of anything from anybody, without a word in his own defense, and they never talked about it again.

Weeks later, Ryan heard the rest of the story from an eyewitness. It turned out the other guy in the fight was telling everybody who'd listen that Fugazzi didn't get enough credit for the football team's success because of that Ryan guy, who was an over-rated stiff.

Ryan couldn't have known it, because Fugazzi would never let on, not even to get the captain off his back.

But the Fonz had been fighting for him.

There was plenty of opportunity for trouble when New Dorp took the boat back to Brooklyn to play New Utrecht High School the second week of the 1959 season, two days after the Los Angeles Dodgers, those traitors, finished beating the "Go-Go" White Sox in a rare World Series that didn't include the Yankees.

If the Centrals handled the Dutchmen as if they knew what was coming, it was because they did.

In the days before football coaches at every level started staying up nights to break down film, most high school scouting was done by word-of-mouth, or by memory. But the week before the New Utrecht game Joe Ryan, Marty's older brother who was playing Army ball at Fort Dix, an hour's drive down the New Jersey Turnpike, gave Somma a detailed scouting report.

Somma's first love was offense, and he spent the bulk of practice working on that phase of the game. But for once, Milza didn't have to sprint from his last-period class and beat Somma to the field to find practice time for the defense.

"We were always prepared," Danny Boylan said. "But not like this. We had their formations, their plays, everything. They never had a chance."

Fugazzi scored three touchdowns, and caused a pair of fumbles on defense. Ryan scored twice, and New Dorp won its second game in as many weeks, 36-8.

The only scary moment for the Centrals came when little Artie Truscelli, the surprise star of New Dorp's opening-day win against Lafayette, got kneed in the head going after a fumble, and knocked cold.

He was unconscious for what seemed like a long time; long enough for Somma and Milza and Tex Dawson, the white-haired trainer who didn't move as quickly as he once might've, to get out there before Truscelli opened his eyes.

For the first time in school history, the New Dorp kids were wearing white jerseys instead of green and gold; shirts purchased for an upcoming appearance on ABC's New York *"High School Game of the Week,"* because two teams in dark-colored jerseys wouldn't make for much of a show on all those black-and-white sets.

When he woke up, the first thing Truscelli saw was the unfamiliar shirts.

"What team am I on?" he asked Tex Dawson.

As the score mounted, the game turned nasty, with several

near-fights on the field, and a few more in the stands.

After the officials broke up yet another scuffle, Fugazzi, who rarely said anything in the huddle, spoke up.

"The next guy who starts a fight," he said, "will finish it with me."

And that was the end of the fighting for that day.

13

Keeper of the Flame

For the New Dorp kids, even home games were away games.

Over the years, with no bleachers at their rocky practice field, and no fence separating the field from the neighborhood of neat, single-family homes that bordered the high school, the Centrals played their "home" games at Thompson's Stadium and Wagner College. But the Stapes' old home, where Red Grange once dressed in a shed with no hot water and the Giants played every Thanksgiving, had succumbed to old age and neglect; by 1959 it was little more than a rubble-strewn lot. And once Wagner added soccer to its roster of fall sports, it was a rare Saturday when the college field wasn't in use.

New Dorp moved its home games to Port Richmond High School, which hadn't fielded a football team of its own in almost 30 years, since the days when Bill Shakespeare played there, on his way to Notre Dame. But Port Richmond still had a field with a concrete grandstand that stretched from end zone to end zone, and could easily accommodate 3,000 fans.

The problem, if you were a New Dorp football player, was that Port Richmond was seven miles away, on the other side of the Island; and there was no money in the school budget for busses to home games.

The driving age in New York was 18, same as the legal drinking age; only a few of the New Dorp kids were old enough to have a driver's license, or access to a car. If a player couldn't get a ride from a parent, or a friend … no sure thing at a time when there were more families on Staten Island who didn't own a car than there were two-car households … it meant getting to the game by bus. Two busses, really; one to the ferry terminal, the Island's transportation hub, and another from the terminal to the field, while wrangling a duffel bag full of equipment.

But wherever they played, the Centrals drew a crowd.

Not many high school kids had year-round jobs in 1959, when it wasn't uncool to stand up and cheer for your school team. And their classmates weren't off playing games of their own. There was no soccer team at New Dorp, no lacrosse or wrestling or volleyball, and no girls' sports at all, unless you counted the cheerleaders.

With a single college football game on television most weekends — and none during the week — Americans looked for entertainment in their own backyards. And with only two high school teams on the Island, and Curtis lucky to break even most years, it wasn't unusual for kids from other schools … especially the jocks, who knew some of the New Dorp players from baseball or basketball … to follow the Centrals around the city, taking the ferry to Manhattan and hopping subways and busses to get to Far Rockaway or Flushing, or some other speck on the map they'd never seen before. With luck, they might see somebody they knew at the game, and get a ride home.

"It was like we were Staten Island's team," Joe Avena said.

"Wherever you went on the Island, you felt like everybody was your friend."

But not everybody went to the games.

Avena's father never saw him play.

Carmine Avena was still a teenager when he left his parents, three brothers, two sisters, and a fourth unborn brother he'd never see in Quaglietta, Italy, and climbed aboard the steamship *Italia* in nearby Naples, bound for an uncertain future in a country where he didn't know the customs or the language.

He had little education, and for the rest of his life he never read a book or owned a library card, never went to a Broadway play or a ballgame or flew in a plane. For most of his adult life he shined other people's shoes from dawn to dusk, six days a week, at the Woolworth Building in Manhattan.

He never called in sick, never took a vacation, and never saw his Italian family again, except for his brother Vito, who was conscripted into the Italian Army at the start of World War Two, captured by American troops, and shipped to a prisoner-of-war camp in Oregon for the duration of the war. It took Carmine Avena four days to get across the country by train. He and his brother shook hands, talked for awhile in Italian. Then Carmine took the train back across the country, and back to the new family he'd built in America.

The Avenas didn't drive, didn't own a car, and didn't have a TV until young Joe was a teenager. But he never felt deprived.

"I knew my parents loved me," he said. "They didn't know anything about football, or American sports … it just wasn't important to them … but they gave me the freedom to do what I wanted to do.

"As long as it was safe, and legal, it was OK."

What he wanted, more than anything, was to play sports. He played all the American games, which on Staten Island and everywhere else in the 1950s meant baseball, football and basketball. Across the cultural divide that separated them, father and son debated the merits of professional wrestling. Carmine Avena rooted for Antonino Rocca and Bruno Sammartino, the Italian stars of the day.

"It's all fake," Joe said.

His father didn't buy it.

Joe was in the first grade when the Avenas moved from Hell's Kitchen, the melting-pot Manhattan neighborhood romanticized on Broadway in "West Side Story," to New Dorp Beach, a colony of bungalows stacked side-by-side on streets so narrow the neighbors had to park with two wheels on the curb, just so cars could get by.

He grew up playing made-up games in the street, learning to root for the Yankees and the football Giants in the days when New York had three baseball teams and every 12-year-old could recite the lineups from memory. In those days, before the big box stores and the shopping strips started going up on that part of the Island, you could look to the west and see the high school, the tallest building in the area, peeking over the tops of the trees, a half-mile away.

Avena was playing stickball in the street that October afternoon in 1951 when somebody's mother burst out of the house with the news that Bobby Thomson, who every kid in the neighborhood knew was a Staten Island guy just like them, hit the home run that beat the Dodgers in their National League playoff. And a few years after that the Avenas moved again, from the beach to the other side of Hylan Boulevard, where there was more room between the houses, and nobody had to worry about the waters of the bay coming up the street when there was a high tide and a full moon.

Joe was in the PS 41 schoolyard across the street — he spent a lot of time in the schoolyard playing basketball or stickball, or arguing about who was better, Mickey Mantle, Willie Mays or

Duke Snider — the first time his friend Ralph Sicurenza stopped to ask if he was going to something Sicurenza called "the Turkey Day game."

"I didn't know what he was talking about," Avena said.

By the time he was a high school freshman, he knew he wanted to play basketball and baseball. He wasn't as sure about football. He started going to the football games with some of the New Dorp basketball players, a group that included Jim Albus, a lanky rebounder and scorer who discovered golf when he got to college, and wound up a six-time winner on the Senior Tour. By the time he was a junior in high school, Albus was a seasoned traveler, having learned to drop from an overpass onto the roof of a Staten Island Rapid Transit train on his way to Cromwell Center, the pier-top recreation center that was a magnet for basketball players of all ages. He'd ride the whole way up there, smiling at passersby who did a double-take when they spotted the blond boy squatting atop his basketball on the roof of a speeding train.

"I only missed one football game that season," Avena said. "That was the day my uncle took me to see the Yankees play the Dodgers in the World Series.

"Enos Slaughter hit a home run."

When New Dorp rallied to beat Curtis on Thanksgiving and finished the season undefeated, marching down the field in the final minutes the way Somma predicted they would, Avena was in the stands with his younger brother, savoring every minute of it.

"The whole thing turned me on to playing," he said.

On the first day of practice the next fall, he found himself in a two-on-one drill matched against Marty Ryan and Fred Fugazzi, a combination so lethal that by the time they were seniors, Somma wouldn't allow Ryan, Fugazzi or Vic Esposito to pair up in drills, unless they were going against each other.

Times like that, Avena knew, it didn't matter if you won or lost, because nobody expected you to win. What mattered was that you didn't quit; that you risked a fat lip ... or humiliation ... and showed the man in the fedora that there was something inside you he could nurture, and build on, until you were one of the guys he called to the front of the bus before a big game. Until you were somebody to be depended upon, which was everything.

"I think the thing that saved me," he said, "was I knew it couldn't get any tougher after that."

He played three sports all the way though high school, and into college. Later in life, one of his few regrets was not putting up more of a fight when an assistant principal decided he couldn't continue to play all three seasons and serve as student-organization president. But he was never as strong as Vic Esposito or Marty Ryan, or a natural athlete like Danny Boylan or little Artie Truscelli. "Everything he did," Boylan said, "to be successful, he worked at it.

"Even then, he was that guy."

He bounced from tight end to blocking back to tailback as a sophomore, when a flu epidemic swept the Island in the middle of the football season and a dozen New Dorp players got sick, including the starting tailback and his back-up.

"We'll close ranks," Somma told them, one of his favorite expressions at times like that. "We'll play even if we have to play Avena at tailback."

Before the start of the next season, Somma sought him out. "You're probably not going to play much at tailback," he told Avena, another of those times when Somma put a suggestion in somebody's head, and let them think it was their idea. "Why don't you try center?"

Avena found his niche as the center in the Single Wing, where every play began with a direct snap to the tailback or fullback, moving targets 4½ yards behind the line of scrimmage.

"How was that?" he'd ask as they went back to the huddle after every play, even though he'd just put the ball on the thigh pad of the back's lead leg, just like the snap before that, and the hundred before that.

Maybe it figured that the guy who cared that much would wind up a coach himself, and the caretaker of Somma's legacy.

When Paul Milza, who always seemed more comfortable as Somma's trusted lieutenant than he did as a head coach, followed his old boss into retirement, Avena returned to New Dorp as the school's head football coach. Then he stayed, long after he and his wife moved to New Jersey and had kids who needed more of him than a head coach has time to give, until he could pass the torch to another of Somma's guys.

With Avena in charge, New Dorp won one last city championship in 1985, the school's first title in 20 years. But the neighborhood had changed, and the high school had changed with it. The tough Italian and Irish kids who played football for Somma in the 1950s and 60s moved on, or they moved up, leaving behind aging parents and grandparents. Zoning changes brought a new wave of immigrants from Africa, the Caribbean, and Eastern Europe, kids who had little interest in football, and no connection to the high school's rich athletic history. But Avena was reluctant to leave when the program was suffering, even though he ached to be home with Linda and the kids.

"I don't know if somebody from another school would understand," he said. "New Dorp was such a big part of my life.

"Fred, Vic, Danny Boylan, Marty Ryan ... they were close to me. And I could go anywhere around New York or New Jersey and they knew New Dorp and Somma. They didn't know me, but they knew New Dorp and Somma.

"To think that I could go back and coach at a place where he established such a tradition ... where I played with so many great players, who were better than I was ... just to be in that position and say you're not going to do that your whole life is a tough thing to sort out."

He had a daughter who played soccer in high school, and he never saw her play, never saw anything she did, and one day he woke up and she was getting ready to go to college. He had a son growing through adolescence, and a wife who rarely got time to talk to him alone during football season, when he'd get home at 10 at night and the phone would ring, and they wouldn't find time that night, either.

"I put that other stuff ahead of my family for a long time, and it was tearing at me," he told a friend. "Just once, I wanted to see them celebrate something with me there."

The way Avena looked at it, football had given him the best friends a man could hope to have. It gave him a calling, gave him role models like Somma and Milza, and a foot in the door at every job he'd ever had, including the one where he met his wife.

Even when it looked like he had nothing as a kid, it turned out he had everything he needed.

"It was a good time," he said. "Life was simple. We had heroes. We had role models. It seemed like the world changed the five or six years after that, with all the drugs, with Vietnam, the assassination of Kennedy.

"We didn't have any of that.

"You knew what it was to be a kid then ... to root for Mickey Mantle and the Yankees and the Giants ... and to play for New Dorp.

"If you didn't go to practice, what would you do?"

He was standing on the porch of his century-old Victorian home on a wide, tree-lined street in Westfield, N.J., where on game days the streets around the high school were thick with Escalades and BMWs, and Avena coached the children of privilege.

"I wish these kids had what I had," he said.

In the fall of 1959, Avena didn't need to see the television trucks from ABC's *"High School Game of the Week"* broadcast, with onetime Olympic sprinter Marty Glickman doing the play-by-play, or hear the emotion in Somma's voice as he got ready to send them onto the field, to know the Brooklyn Tech game was a big deal.

He remembered walking into the locker room two years earlier, after New Dorp lost to Tech in the first game of his sophomore season.

"All the older guys were crying," he said. "I never saw guys cry like that."

When he was a junior, Tech beat New Dorp again, in a battle of unbeaten teams, the only hiccup for New Dorp in an otherwise perfect season. It was one of those days that taught him ... taught all of them ... that contrary to all the old coaching clichés, the game didn't always go to the team that wanted it the most. Sometimes both teams deserved to win.

This time the Centrals got on top early, and stayed there. Danny Boylan, starting on offense for the first time, caught a short jump pass from Truscelli — the Single Wing version of "play action" — and broke it for a 51-yard touchdown. Then he caught another touchdown pass from Ryan.

Fugazzi ran for over 100 yards for the second straight week, and the defense held Tech to four first downs. Adam Cirillo, the Tech coach, was a former college star at Lafayette, and Somma's friend, but he had a colorful working vocabulary, especially when things were going badly for his team. After listening to Cirillo vent for three quarters, Somma walked down the sideline at Port Richmond, where both benches were on the same side of the field.

"Adam," he shouted, "would you please watch your mouth!"

The whole thing felt more one-sided than 18-7.

Avena, who didn't always get to play defense, was right in the middle of all of it.

When Somma handed him the game ball, he kissed it.

That night, after dinner, Milza's phone rang. It wasn't uncommon for Somma to call on Saturday night after a game, unable to relax until he addressed some flaw he wanted them to work on in practice. But this phone call, three weeks into the season, was different from most of the others.

"Paul," Somma said, "I think we're gonna have a good team this year."

14

The Missing Piece

By the time the last of the leaves had turned, the football season had taken on a familiar rhythm.

On Tuesdays, Wednesdays and Thursdays, the days when everybody hoped they wouldn't wind up paired against Fred Fugazzi, Marty Ryan or Vic Esposito in a hitting drill, the New Dorp kids beat up on each other.

Fridays were like a dress rehearsal, when they turned out in their game uniforms, right down to the striped socks and the fat, gold shoelaces the student-managers handed out before the first game. Then on Saturday they went out and beat up on the other guys, the way they'd rehearsed it. That night, they'd celebrate with a party at one of the cheerleaders' houses, the way they imagined the Giants did at Toots Shor's saloon, or one of those swanky East Side steakhouses in the city.

But none of it was routine for Artie Truscelli, New Dorp's talented and impulsive tailback, who had never played on a team where everybody had matching pants, shirts and helmets, and a number to call their own.

The neighborhood teams he played on did the best they could, mixing and matching. "Sometimes they'd get a deal on uniforms," he said. "The only problem was half the guys would be wearing number 83, and the other half would be wearing 88."

Somehow, Truscelli had managed to remain academically ineligible his first three years in high school.

He never got into any real trouble, unless you counted sneaking down to Great Kills Park for a couple of beers, or camping out in the woods overnight and raiding the boxes of donuts sitting outside the A&P the next morning, before the store opened.

"If I got in real trouble," he said, "my older brothers would've kicked my ass."

And it's not like he couldn't do the work.

He was in Italian class one day when Concettina Brunno, a young language teacher, asked who could tell her how a debate worked. Truscelli raised his hand.

"It's when da fisherman puts da bait on da hook."

After class, she asked why a sharp guy like him wasn't doing better in school. And after that, he did ... at least in her class.

"She put it in a nice way," he said. "She didn't push.

"And besides, she was pretty."

And that was it in a nutshell. Whenever somebody pushed ... when they tried to tell him what he should be doing, or tried to lead him by the hand .... Truscelli went the other way.

"If I knew me when I was a kid," he said, "I'd give myself a beating every night."

When his friend Jimmy Killeen tried to sell him on the idea of going out for football, Truscelli shrugged him off in a way that suggested he was too cool to care.

The truth was he'd been to the high school games, and seen the way the crowds reacted when the New Dorp kids came out in their yellow helmets and the shirts with the stripes on the sleeves ... especially on Thanksgiving, when it seemed like everybody on Staten Island was at the game, and New Dorp always won.

"Like a professional game," he said.

"I didn't think I was good enough."

He was playing for a sandlot team called the Staten Island Tigers at Semler's Park, the picnic ground where old man Semler cut a hole in the fence to make it easier for the Ryan brothers to get to the field. After the Tigers' last game, Somma, who'd been watching, walked over and told Truscelli he ought to come out for the high school team.

"You'll have to get your grades up," Somma told him, a sign he'd already done his homework on Truscelli.

"I figured he needed some extra guys," Truscelli said.

What Somma needed was a passer.

In its purest form, the Single Wing was a power-running offense, designed to get double-team blocks and superior numbers at the point of attack. But Charlie Caldwell, the Princeton coach who jazzed up the old formation by adding a split end and men-in-motion, had demonstrated how a true double-threat tailback like 1951 Heisman Trophy winner Dick Kazmaier, who was as likely to throw the ball as run with it, could keep a defense on its heels. Sometimes the threat of the pass was as effective as the real thing.

Somma had other kids who could throw the ball if he asked. Marty Ryan could throw it, and Fred Fugazzi could throw it in a pinch. But as the blocking back, where he was like another pulling guard, Ryan had limited opportunities; and throwing the ball wasn't what Fugazzi did best.

And none of them threw it like Truscelli.

He was 5-7 and 135 pounds, tops, and even in pads and a helmet it looked like half those 67 inches were neck. But despite his size, or lack of it, Truscelli was a natural athlete, and he'd been playing baseball and football in choose-up games and in the sandlot leagues, where he could hone his competitive instincts, from the time he was old enough to follow one of his older brothers to the nearest vacant lot.

"They'd put me in the outfield until one of the big kids came," he said. "Then they'd chuck me.

"Nobody ever knew where I was, but in those days that was OK."

The transition to high school ball wasn't always smooth. Somma wasn't a fan of ad-libs. "Everything was organized," Truscelli said. "And I was a wing-it type of guy." And there was the question of his grades, which turned out to be not that big a problem.

"It was something I wanted," he said. "So I started doing my homework."

It turned out size didn't matter much, either. "I was afraid they were all going to be giants," Truscelli said. "And they were, compared to me. But I had Marty on one side of me in the huddle and Freddie on the other side, telling me 'Nice play!' The confidence they gave me made it easy."

In his first scrimmage, he came flying up from his safety position on defense and cracked a bigger ballcarrier. "What a hit!" Somma enthused, raising a fist in the air the way he did when he was excited. And even if, as Truscelli later suspected, Somma was only trying to pump him up, it worked.

He could do this.

But it was when he threw the ball that he got everybody's attention. In practice, the Centrals split into two lines of backs and receivers running pass patterns, and sometimes they'd count along as he threw one strike after another "... five ... six ... seven ..." until he missed one.

Some days he completed 20 or 30 in a row before he overthrew a receiver on a deep ball ... "Never Dennis Tancredi, he used to out-run the ball" ... or somebody muffed a square-out, one of those patterns where he tried to throw the ball where only the receiver had a chance to catch it.

And once the games started, it was obvious that Truscelli was the missing piece in the puzzle Somma had been putting together in his head since before the previous season was over.

His favorite target was Danny Boylan, his pitch-and-catch teammate from the sandlots. Long before anybody got around to keeping track of "yards after the catch," Truscelli developed a knack for throwing a soft, catchable ball where Boylan could grab it in stride, and turn short passes into big plays.

"He was a big target, easy to see," Truscelli said. "I could throw a bad pass, and he'd still catch it."

He didn't throw many bad ones. New Dorp had never been a big passing team, but in the Centrals' first three games Truscelli threw for five touchdowns; and if opposing linebackers and safeties sat back, protecting against the pass, Fugazzi, Ryan and Truscelli ran over them, or around them.

Football didn't give him a calling, the way it did for Joe Avena, or a blueprint for life, the way it would for Vic Esposito. It took 27 years on the Fire Department to do that. Truscelli got on the job at the last possible moment, when he was 31, long after he passed up a chance to follow Fugazzi to college at Missouri Valley ... one more time when he was reluctant to step outside his comfort zone ... and spent a decade working a variety of construction jobs.

He was a natural for the Fire Department; a lean bundle of fast-twitch muscle who could cook, sing, and tell from a whiff of smoke before the rig turned the last corner if they were on their way to a structure fire, a car fire, or a grease fire. He would've stayed on the job longer if he hadn't fallen through the floor of a burning building, and torn the cartilage in his hip.

Funny how it turned out. All those years of swimming against the tide, rebelling against authority, and the best times of his life were the ones he spent as part of a team: the 27 years with the FDNY, and the one season on Sal Somma's football team, with Marty Ryan standing on one side of him and Fred Fugazzi on the other, and Joe Avena coming back to the huddle after every snap, asking "How was that?"

"Everybody was like a brother," he said. "They looked after you."

A lot had changed since the first time a New Dorp football team took the 69th St. Ferry to play Lincoln in the fall of 1949, when Somma's "farmers" showed the Brooklyn kids they could play football.

A month into the 1959 season, New Dorp was the only undefeated public-school team in the city.

Against Lincoln, Truscelli ran for two more touchdowns and threw for a third, accounting for all the scoring in a 20-0 victory, before he left the game with a bruised hip.

"I got a little cocky, and stopped avoiding guys," he said.

"I got so pumped up, I thought I was Freddie."

15

You Don't Juke Victor

The first Saturday in November, with their perfect record and a playoff berth on the line, a bunch of the New Dorp kids were late getting to Port Richmond for a game against Thomas Jefferson, the kind of thing that hardly ever happened on Somma's watch.

On mornings when the Centrals had a home game, Fugazzi, Truscelli, Barchitta, and Charlie Langere met at Pete Chiapperini's house, and Pete's mother fed them hotdogs for breakfast. Then they threw their equipment bags into Fugazzi's '49 Dodge for the ride to Port Richmond High School.

Somehow, when they were wedging themselves into the car, Fugazzi's loose-leaf binder wound up on the fender.

When he turned the corner, the book slid off its perch, bounced once on the pavement, and skittered to the curb. Loose papers floated on the breeze, and a ripple of nervous laughter escaped from the back seat.

"You think it's funny?" Fugazzi growled, hitting the brakes.

"We're not goin' anywhere until every page is back where it belongs."

His teammates knew that tone. Within seconds, they were out of the car, hunting down errant pieces of paper.

Fugazzi waited until they were back in the car. Then he took his time assessing the damage, letting them squirm. By the time they got to Port Richmond, the rest of the team was dressed and ready to go on the field for warm-ups.

Tom O'Connor, who'd become a regular member of New Dorp's game-day entourage, helping Tex Dawson tape ankles and dispensing his own brand of locker-room humor, met them at the gate. He was an elementary school teacher, after-school playground director and baseball umpire, good enough to work a few Yankee games when the major-league umpires went on strike. O'Connor wasn't easily thrown off his game. But now he was clearly agitated.

"Where the hell have you guys been?"

Somma was waiting at the locker room door. If he was amused, he hid it well.

"He benched everybody but Fred," Barchitta said.

By the end of the first quarter, Somma relented. "All right, you jugheads," he told the contrite latecomers, "get in there."

But by then, Vic Esposito had already blown up the Thomas Jefferson center, and the game.

The last guy to play high school football in New York City without a facemask wasn't always the biggest, baddest kid on the block.

Esposito grew up in Rosebank, riding shotgun in his father's truck when they went to buy produce at farms on the South Shore, stopping to look at the cows at Mount Loretto. They'd park on the side of the road, and sell cucumbers and fat, ripe tomatoes out of the back of the truck. On warm summer evenings, when Vic and his pre-adolescent buddies were bored, they'd sneak up to the parked cars down at Penny Beach, where young lovers went to look at the moon. They'd knock on the windows, and laugh all the way up the block as they ran away.

His family had lived in the neighborhood since an aunt was diagnosed with tuberculosis. "They told her she should move to a country setting," Vic said. "So they came to Staten Island."

In the Fall of 1955, Esposito joined a sandlot football team coached by his older brother; the kind of neighborhood team that practiced under the streetlights in front of St. Mary's Elementary School, and scrounged up pants and helmets wherever they could, to go with the shirts supplied by the LaMattina Brothers lumber yard.

It was a weight-limit league, a measure enforced with weekly weigh-ins at Earl's Sports Shop in Stapleton, the kind of place where a guy could go into a booth and listen to an Elvis Presley record before he decided if he wanted to buy it, or go down into the basement and swing a baseball bat for as long as he wanted, without having to worry about breaking up the furniture.

For a kid, a visit to Earl's was always an adventure. But on one of his weekly trips to Stapleton, Esposito was appalled to learn he weighed a few pounds over the league limit.

"What time do you close?" he asked the guy manning the scales.

"Five o'clock."

"I'll be back," Esposito said, and he crossed the street to the little park that anchored the shopping district, where he ran laps between the pigeons and the benches until 4:55. When he got back to the store, he was legal again.

Most of his LaMattina Brothers teammates were recent high school graduates. Some of them had played for Somma at New Dorp, and by the standards of the neighborhood they were pretty good; good enough to win the first-half league championship. But when the season stretched past Thanksgiving, they loaded up for the championship game by adding a couple of the high school players who had just finished their season the way they usually did at New Dorp, by beating Curtis.

Everybody in the tight-knit community of Rosebank knew Essy Curatolo and Don Rizzo, a high school star on his way to the University of Tennessee. But to make room on the roster for the new guys, somebody had to go. So Lou Esposito cut his little brother.

"I couldn't believe it," Vic said. "His own brother!"

It gave him little comfort, then, that he was only in the eighth grade, not that far removed from the time his brother brought home a pair of shoulder pads that looked like wings, and convinced young Vic that if he put them on, and ran fast enough, he could fly.

"I ran around the house all day," Vic said. "But I could never get off the ground."

He didn't get off to a fast start in school, either. The nuns kept him back in first grade, and again in second grade, and after that his parents took him out of St. Mary's and put him in the public school up the street, and he did fine. But from the first time he heard Somma talk … when he heard the passion in his voice, and knew it was coming straight from his heart … it was as if Esposito had been waiting his whole life for that moment; waiting for somebody to lay out a game plan for living the way this humble man in the suit and tie was doing it.

"He made you better than you were," Esposito said.

"I never experienced a guy who could do that. I think maybe Lombardi might've had that. All of a sudden, I found myself staying up at night, studying. I never did that before. He made me want to reach for more than just football. There's no way you could play for him and not come away a better person.

"He'd talk about the players who were there before you got there, and the sacrifices they made. It made you feel like you wanted to bring it up a notch.

"You wanted to be one of those guys he talked about.

"I thank the Lord I got that opportunity."

It almost didn't happen. At the start of his sophomore year at New Dorp, the Espositos saw a chance to own a house of their own, after years of renting. They moved across the Island, to a neighborhood where the high school kids went to Curtis, or they went to St. Peter's, the parish school known for its basketball teams, where they didn't even have a football team. For months, he expected somebody to knock on the door and tell him he was going to have to transfer. "Nobody said anything," he said. "And I didn't want to tell anybody.

"After that first year went by, I figured I was in the clear."

From the first day, he was like a sponge whenever Somma was talking, whether he was showing the offensive linemen how to pull out of the line to lead a play ... "He'd spend an hour on that first step" ... or delivering homespun essays on life. *The hard way is the easy way.*" Esposito soaked it all up, took it to heart, and packed it away in a place where he could hit re-dial whenever he needed it.

"So much of my life has been built on what I got from Sal Somma," he said. "It's always amazing to me how many people are just winging it."

The way Esposito heard it, Somma's approach to football, which turned out to be just as applicable to running a modeling agency or selling real estate, went like this: First you had to understand what you needed to do to be successful. Then you practiced it, and practiced it some more ... "You learn to do by doing," he used to say ... until it was second nature, and you could do it without thinking about it.

Then you could call yourself a football player.

"It's not complicated," Esposito said. "It's really pretty simple.

"You just gotta do it."

Esposito could call himself a football player. He was good enough to start at North Carolina on a team that lost its second game of the season at Michigan State and won nine of the other 10, including a 35-0 wipeout of Air Force in the Gator Bowl. After a couple of years bouncing from the Canadian Football League to the Continental Football League, he was one of the Jets' last cuts in the fall of 1968, the season they made good on Joe Namath's guarantee by upsetting the Colts in the Super Bowl. If Weeb Ewbank didn't bring in six-time all-star Bob Talamini at the last minute to beef up the offensive line, Esposito might've wound up with a ring.

His older brother was a better-than-average high school player, and lost his chance at a college scholarship when he took a job on the docks and got sick working in the holds of the big ships. But it never occurred to Esposito that he was playing for a scholarship, or a shot at pro money.

"I just had a deep love for the game," he said. "I loved to be in the middle of it.

"It was almost like a high, getting in there and mixing it up."

He played right from the start at New Dorp, unfazed as a freshman playing with all those upperclassmen, after his time banging heads with the older guys in the Earl's Sport Shop league. Marty Ryan remembered watching him play the Curtis game that first year on a knee that was swollen the size of a basketball.

Facemasks had only recently come into vogue in high school. Ben Sarullo, the New Dorp captain when Esposito was a sophomore, never wore a mask. He broke his nose in three straight Thanksgiving Day games against Curtis.

After trying it as a sophomore, Esposito decided a facemask only got in his way. But he wasn't entirely reckless; he wore a protective cup, and when he was getting undressed after a game one Saturday he saw his cup was cracked in half. When he thought about what might've happened if he hadn't been wearing it, he broke into a sweat.

He was an All-City offensive tackle, a 6-foot-1, 210-pound blend of power and technique before anybody knew much about weight training, when that was big for a high school kid, and he made an offensive line of otherwise average size and ability — Avena, Pete Chiapperini, Matt Cavallo, Bob Johnson and ends Bill Chambers and Danny Boylan — something more than ordinary. "I loved to double-team with him," Boylan said. "He'd have the guy all set up. I'd just lean into him, and it would be over."

"He always did things the way they should be done."

He was quick enough that Somma experimented with using him as a tight end, until the day the team was watching film when a clip came up showing Esposito looking away as the ball hit his hands. "This is how you *don't* do it," Somma told them, and after that Esposito went back to knocking people down, although Somma did put in a "tackle-eligible" play designed for him.

When they talked about using the play against Brooklyn Tech, Esposito was so eager that he came back to the huddle early in the game, and told Ryan he was open.

"How do you know you're open?" Ryan said. "We haven't run the play yet."

But it was on defense, where he was a noseguard — neutralizing the center before he could get out of his stance, and then finding the ballcarrier — that Esposito was a destructive force.

Every defender, one time or another, has been told to keep his eyes on a ballcarrier's belly button, because no matter how the slickest runner feints or fakes, his mid-section's not going anywhere. Like most sideline instructions, it's easier said than done. But Esposito was such a sure tackler that when Bob Ryan joined the team, Marty warned his younger brother, "You don't juke Victor."

"He was made to play that position," Ryan said.

Besides being the best two-way lineman in the city, the kid who was left back by the nuns at St. Mary's was a National Honor Society member and student-body president — the kind of solid citizen Mary McGinnis, the dignified high school principal, had in mind when she brought Somma back from Vermont to be a role model for her football team — and as tough as he had to be in a game that was only half-civilized.

When they were juniors, Avena was filling in at tight end alongside Esposito, who was lined up opposite a big defensive lineman who'd been running his mouth since the opening kick-off.

Late in the game, as Esposito settled into his stance, the other guy was still talking. He was in mid-sentence, just before the snap, when Esposito looked up and spit in his face.

Then he put the big kid on his back.

"Vic didn't do much talking," Avena said.

"Once that ball was snapped," Paul Barchitta said, "he was a different person."

The kids from Thomas Jefferson found out all about that.

Thomas Jefferson High School was in East New York, a gritty Brooklyn neighborhood where mothers brought their sons by the hand to football coach Moe Finkelstein, knowing that for the next four years they'd have direction and purpose in their lives, and come home too tired to go looking for trouble.

Led by all-city fullback Larry Bernstein, Jefferson had the highest-scoring offense in the city, averaging 30 points a game. But the first time they had to punt against New Dorp, the Jefferson center, his head ringing from one of Esposito's head slaps, was in such a hurry to defend himself that he snapped the ball over the punter's head. New Dorp took advantage of the short field, and three plays later Fugazzi fell into the end zone for the first touchdown of the day.

The next time Jefferson got the ball, Esposito spooked the same kid into another wild snap, and New Dorp got another cheap touchdown for a quick 14-0 lead.

"That was Vic," Joe Avena said. "He intimidated people."

The game wasn't going to be that easy. The Jefferson center, having decided he was more afraid of Moe Finkelstein than he was of Esposito, regained his composure. The Jeffs, rocked back on their heels, came back to tie the game and turn it into a war, before New Dorp put together two long scoring drives in the second half, and hung on to win 28-22.

When it was over … leaving the Centrals drained and tested, but still the only undefeated team in the city, their dream season still intact heading into the playoffs … Paul Barchitta wanted to know why there was so much cheering.

After showing up late with the rest of Fugazzi's carload of captive passengers, Barchitta got into the game in time to take the brunt of a head-on collision with Bernstein that left him dazed in the dirt, and he played most of the final quarter in a haze.

"I was so punchy, I thought the game was tied," he said.

16

Dan Boylan's Kid

It was just another practice play, the one that gave Somma an excuse to get Danny Boylan into the starting lineup; one more in a succession of plays the Centrals would run over and over in practice until the coach was satisfied everybody was on the same page, except this time Artie Truscelli saw his first two receivers were covered. Instinctively, he turned to the other side of the formation and lofted a perfect spiral in the direction of Lou Miceli, his split end, who was running a deep flag pattern.

"Chick" Miceli was a sharp kid, popular in the hallways at New Dorp, part of all the boys-will-be-boys horseplay in the locker room, and one of a small circle of humans who could tweak Fred Fugazzi and get away with it. Years later, he made a bundle on Wall Street. But on this day, for this one play, he was going through the motions, jogging at half-speed with his head down, not expecting the ball to come his way.

"Chickie!" somebody started to yell, the warning dying in his throat.

Too late.

Somma, who abhorred sloppiness almost as much as he hated laziness, was shaking his head as he advanced on Truscelli.

"Why'd you throw the ball there?" he asked, a question that must've sounded like an accusation to Truscelli, who explained that nobody else was open.

Somma turned his attention downfield.

"Miceli, you jughead," he said, "why weren't you going full speed?"

Chickie's explanation ... that Truscelli never threw to him on that play ... didn't begin to satisfy Somma.

"Boylan!" he called, turning on his heel, "... get in there at end." And from that point forward, whenever Somma announced the starting lineup, the way he did in the locker room before each game "... and starting today, at center ...." Danny Boylan was the split end, on the other end of the line from Billy Chambers, his buddy going all the way back to the first grade at Our Lady Queen of Peace elementary school.

Chambers lived three blocks from the high school, the kind of proximity that led to a casual approach toward punctuality. On school days, he tended to linger in bed or over breakfast until the last possible moment, then bolt out the back door and through the neighboring yards in a dash to beat the late bell and avoid the attention of Sol Feinberg. The New Dorp attendance officer sometimes ordered habitual offenders to stand at attention with their arms out to the side, holding a heavy textbook in each hand, until beads of sweat appeared on their foreheads, and their arms began to quiver. But despite Feinberg's best efforts, some habits died hard.

"Even when I got to college, I had to pay guys to get me up early," Chambers said.

He was a big, genial kid, the kind Somma might've spotted in gym class, and encouraged to come out for football. But when Chambers was eight years old he had rheumatic fever, which left him with a heart murmur, and left his doctors and parents with reservations about exposing him to strenuous activities.

All through grade school, he wasn't allowed to play sports, or even ride a bike. As a high school freshman, he worked out with the football team but didn't participate in games or contact drills, while doctors monitored his health. But once he was cleared to play, his father handed him over with specific instructions.

"Give the kid a kick in the ass," he told Somma. "Make a man out of him."

Bill Chambers Sr. was a New York harbor pilot, part of a small fraternity of men who climbed oily rope ladders up the heaving side of massive freighters and cruise ships in rolling seas, and guided them through fog, wind, and shifting tides to the relative safety of the inner harbor.

In a neighborhood where a city job meant financial security, the chance to join a closed shop like the harbor pilots, where most rookies had to be blood relatives just to get a foot in the door, was like winning the lottery. But Bill Chambers had been going to sea, in one fashion or another, since he was 12, when he started working on the tugboats. He'd seen the hard side of life, and the old salt wasn't an easy man to please.

"If I got 90 on a test, I should've got 100," his son said. "When I started playing football, I guess he liked that. I found out later in life that he used to brag about me, but he'd never tell me.

"There could be 5,000 people in the stands at Port Richmond, and I'd hear his voice: 'Jesus Christ! Did you miss that tackle?'

"I guess he wanted to make me a better person, even though sometimes I wanted to whack him."

It wasn't until the old man was dead that Chambers found the scrapbooks in the attic, the ones full of yellowed newspaper clippings about his games, and the notations in his father's hand ... "Junior did good" ... scribbled in the margins.

"God forbid he ever said any of it to me," Chambers said.

All along, Danny Boylan was the one telling Chambers he should play football at New Dorp.

It just took Boylan a little longer to get there.

He was 6-2, with soft hands and a nose for the ball, the kind of instinct that can't be taught.

But until he started catching touchdown passes for the high school team, he was better known as Dan Boylan's kid.

Everybody on that part of the Island knew Dan Boylan, who worked for Borough President Joseph Palma. He was on his way home from Borough Hall one day in the fall of 1938 when he stopped to watch some neighborhood kids playing at Gillies Field, which was little more than a vacant lot along the railroad tracks, next to the coal yard.

The New Dorp Queens took their name from Our Lady Queen of Peace, the Catholic church up the block. All the rest of it, apparently, they'd been making up as they went along. After watching awhile, Boylan strolled into the huddle and asked if he could offer a suggestion or two.

By the end of the afternoon, the Queens had a new coach.

As a sandlot coach, Boylan was ahead of his time, corresponding with some of the top college coaches in the country, and using spread formations before the pros got around to that kind of thing. And as good as he was as a coach, everybody who knew him agreed he was a better person, a father figure to half the kids in the neighborhood.

Over the next 14 seasons, as those kids grew into men, the Queens went looking for the best competition they could find, and won everywhere they played. Five times they went through the season undefeated, and in three of those years they were unbeaten, untied and unscored-upon.

Until Somma showed up and started accumulating championships at the high school, they were the varsity on that part of the Island.

In those years, some of the best athletes in the neighborhood played for the high school team on Saturday, and for the Queens on Sunday. The only difference was the Queens won more games, and drew bigger crowds. So when the Public Schools Athletic League announced its intention to enforce a prohibition against outside ball, most of the New Dorp kids ignored the warning. Ten of them were suspended for the 1944 high school season, and the Centrals went all year without winning a game, same as they had the year before. Meantime the Queens *beat* a high school team, Pope Pius High School in Passaic, N.J. where a crowd of 2,500 fans just assumed the visitors were another school team.

A few years later, when some of those same kids came back from the war, all grown up, the Queens played in what may have been the first night football game on Staten Island. For a young kid tagging along with his father's team, it was all grand stuff.

Then Dan Boylan died.

Dan Jr. was in the seventh grade, the only boy in the family, with three older sisters who doted on their baby brother. "It was like I could do no wrong," he said. "And I took advantage. Then I got to high school ... public school, where you walked from class to class, and if you didn't feel like going, nobody was going to stop you.

"I loved history and geography. But if it was science or math ... I'd be sitting there day-dreaming about playing football for the New York Giants, and there was nobody there to hit me over the head.

"They kind of cut me some slack ... and I ran with it."

He wasn't the only one. Places like Gillies Field and Semler's Park, where the Staten Island Tigers played, were full of playground stars like Boylan and Artie Truscelli and Danny O'Byrne, who could throw a perfect spiral 70 yards in the air, and never played a down of high school ball.

But like Truscelli, somewhere between his junior and senior year Boylan decided he didn't want to spend another football season on the outside looking in.

"I think Mr. Somma might've twisted Miss Baldassano's arm to give me that last passing grade in Earth Science," he said, only a little serious.

By then, every kid in the neighborhood, and some who didn't even live in the high school sending district, wanted to play for New Dorp. In the spring, Somma and Milza would have 100 kids, or 125, come out for football. As the weeks went by, they dropped by the wayside, a few at a time.

"Sal never told anybody they couldn't play," Milza said. "He didn't believe in putting up lists. Kids saw how much work it was, or they saw that maybe they weren't as good as the next guy, and they drifted away."

Right from the start, there was never any doubt Boylan was going to have to play. He was too sure-handed, too quick to the ball for Somma to keep him on the bench. At first he and Milza put Boylan on defense, at safety, where he could read the play and go get the ball, and then Chickie Miceli gave Somma an excuse to get him into the starting lineup.

"Sal was a product of the Depression," Milza said. "You worked for what you wanted.

"He didn't hand out a starting job. What you got, you earned."

Somma wasn't the only one who felt that way. The Centrals were playing two-hand touch in one of their "voluntary" August workouts when Boylan came over the middle for a pass, and

Fugazzi hit him a shot that rattled the new kid's teeth.

"He laid me out," Boylan said. "I remember thinking to myself, 'Why'd he do that?'

"The only thing I could come up with was that he was testing me."

By the time the season started, Boylan had earned everybody's respect, and the Centrals were the beneficiaries of the years he and Truscelli played pitch-and-catch back at Semler's Park, and on a dozen other sandlot fields, playgrounds, and vacant lots. Not that there weren't some bumps in the road.

He came back to the huddle one Friday afternoon when Somma's guys were going through their paces in their game uniforms, like actors at a Broadway dress rehearsal, and sought out Marty Ryan, who called the plays.

"I'm getting jammed a lot," he told Ryan.

Somma, standing just outside the huddle, overheard.

"Dan," he said, "I'd like you to tell Marty when you're going to be open."

"Don't tell him how hard it is to get there."

He got open a lot, and turned a lot of 10-yard passes into 30 and 40-yard touchdowns. On defense, he had a knack for laying off just enough to bait opposing quarterbacks into throwing his way, and then jumping the pass. And on those rare occasions when he didn't sniff out what was coming, the ball seemed to find him, like the time he was straining to break up a pass that was tipped at the last instant, and the ball wound up wedged under his arm.

"I looked down and it was there," he said.

"It was like ... 'Holy Christ, I caught it!'

"This sounds corny," Boylan said, and he looked like he might be getting ready to cry. "I thought my father put it there."

And somewhere along the way, he found something else.

Over the course of that one season of high school football

with Somma and Milza and the teammates who were going to be his friends for life, Danny Boylan found himself.

"It made me really grow up," he was saying 40 years later, retired from a career as a harbor pilot, another part of his life he shared with Billy Chambers, whose father got them both on the job in the days when the pilots ran a closed shop, and you needed to be a blood relative or the next best thing, just to get your foot in the door.

"It made me think about things like responsibility and accountability," Boylan said. "It sounds corny, but it's the truth. I think it gave me a sense of self-assuredness I didn't have before.

"I felt like I was somebody. And maybe before that, I really didn't.

"Aside from getting married and having my kids ... forget the job or anything else ... that one year was probably the most important thing in my life."

By the time the newly minted New York City playoffs rolled around, the public school league's decision to realign its 20 teams according to geography — all the Brooklyn schools and New Dorp in two six-team divisions, everybody else in two four-team divisions — had proven a competitive disaster.

While New Dorp was bumping off a playoff-worthy contender every week, none of the four Manhattan-Bronx division teams could get through their regular-season schedule with a winning record, which left league officials the dubious task of picking a division winner from among three schools with identical 2-3 records. And at least one of the coaches involved, Stuyvesant's Murl Thrush, sounded as if he was ready for the season to be over.

"The way we've been playing lately," Thrush told the *Daily News*, "we couldn't beat a junior high school team. I hope the committee names somebody else champions."

After losing their opener, Andy Barberi's Curtis Warriors surprised everybody by winning three of their next four games, just missing the playoff lineup. But unlike some of the other teams that were left out of the playoffs, the Warriors still had their Thanksgiving Day date with New Dorp to look forward to ... always the game that mattered most on that side of the bay, as long as Barberi had anything to say about it.

League officials took Stuyvesant's Murl Thrush at his word, and named James Monroe High School, the alma mater of baseball Hall of Famer Hank Greenberg, champions of the Manhattan-Bronx division. But New Dorp made short work of the Eagles in their semifinal match-up, even without the passing game that revolved around Artie Truscelli, who still hadn't fully healed from the deep thigh bruise he suffered two weeks earlier.

The Centrals scored the first two times they had the ball, the second time on a 75-yard cross-country run by Fred Fugazzi, who stiff-armed two Monroe defenders into the dirt. Boylan caught a short flip from Marty Ryan on "Running Pass," the play he and Trusecelli had elevated into an art form, and turned it into a 50-yard touchdown.

By halftime, Ryan had emptied out the Single Wing playbook, including a Statue of Liberty play — the great-granddaddy of trick plays, perfected a half-century earlier by Amos Alonzo Stagg at the University of Chicago — which Dennis Tancredi turned into the fourth New Dorp touchdown. After that, the Centrals intercepted four Monroe passes to ice a 34-14 victory, extending their perfect season and wrapping up a berth in New York City's first official championship game.

But while the Centrals were taking care of business, Staten Islanders who didn't go to the game found themselves glued to ABC's *"Game of the Week"* telecast of the other semifinal game, watching on their black-and-white Philcos and Zeniths as

Tilden's Ron Bliey, the city's leading scorer, scored on runs of 97 and 87 yards … and set up his third touchdown of the day with a 47-yard run to the one-yard line … against a Flushing defense that hadn't been scored on in a month.

Don Iasparro, whose family had moved from Brooklyn to Staten Island earlier in the year, went to the New Dorp game with some of his classmates. When he got home that afternoon, fresh from the victory over Monroe, his father and his brother were waiting for him.

"New Dorp's gonna get killed!" they said at once.

17

The Next Jim Brown

The New Dorp kids had been hearing about Ron Bliey since before the season started.

When the bus was early getting to Brooklyn's Samuel Tilden High School for the season opener against Lafayette, the New Dorp players sat in the stands, enjoying the late September sunshine while they waited to get in the locker room. And when the kids from the neighborhood came around to talk, they all wanted to talk about the new guy who'd been running over everybody in Tilden's pre-season scrimmages.

Bliey had come to Brooklyn from Clearwater, Florida, where he made a bunch of all-state teams as a sophomore. He was big, even for a high school fullback, a little over six feet tall and 195 pounds, about the same size as Marty Ryan, and even faster than Tilden halfback Nick Ucci, who finished fourth in the city in the 100-yard dash.

"He's gonna be the next Jim Brown," one of the Tilden kids

said, and pretty soon that phrase started finding its way into the newspapers. In Tilden's first six games, Bliey ran for 1,200 yards and 15 touchdowns, averaging almost 13 yards every time he touched the ball. By the time the championship game rolled around, he was even wearing Brown's number 44.

Tilden's Bernie Mars was an easy-going coach, given to entertaining his players with tales of his undergraduate days at Brooklyn College, where he played alongside Allie Sherman, who had just replaced Vince Lombardi as the Giants' offensive coordinator, and would soon be their head coach. Bliey had worn a different number for each game that season, a superstition that began after an opening-day loss; when he asked to wear 44 in the title game, Mars went out and bought some new shirts, so his star could have the number Jim Brown and Ernie Davis made famous at Syracuse.

Somma, always the master motivator, made certain none of it was lost on his players. Every morning he sent out for the *Times*, the *Daily News*, the *Herald Tribune* and the *Journal American*. By the time the players got to the locker room, a student manager had taped the latest stories to the wall, where nobody could miss them.

In a few short seasons, Bliey would be starting in the backfield at Notre Dame ... "as Ronnie Bliey goes, so go the Irish," one backfield coach predicted ... but for one afternoon, anyway, Somma was determined not to make things easy for him.

"The whole idea seemed to be if you shut down Bliey, you shut down the whole team," Charlie Romanolo said.

"We weren't playing Tilden ... we were playing *him*."

Early in the week, Somma and Milza experimented with a few wrinkles to counter Tilden's option attack, asking defensive ends Billy Chambers and John Samulski to sit and read the play before committing themselves.

On Thursday, the Centrals went back to being who they were.

"Forget all that other stuff," Somma told them. The new plan was simple, direct, knock-somebody-down-and-sort-it-out-later stuff. It was football. *No holds barred.* When the play came their way, Chambers and Samulski would hit Tilden quarterback Bruce Rubin. When Bliey got the ball, which would be most of the time, the defensive halfbacks — nobody had gotten around to calling them cornerbacks — would try to turn the play inside, so the safeties could come up and make the tackle before Bliey got free in the open field.

"If that's not good enough," Somma told his kids, "they can win the game."

Downing Stadium, where 45,000 New Yorkers watched Jesse Owens run on a cinder track in the 1936 Olympic Trials, was a concrete bowl, built as a make-work project in the early days of the Depression. It sat on Randalls Island in the middle of the East River, a place once valued for its isolation, where the city's flotsam and jetsam — drunks, juvenile delinquents, the chronically insane and chronically poor — could be warehoused out of the sight of polite society. Now the stadium sat in the shadow of the elevated roadways leading to the Triborough Bridge, another link in Robert Moses' chain of highways linking the five boroughs to one another, and the city to the suburbs. But it wasn't the distant rumble of traffic that caught the Centrals' attention in the anxious moments before the championship game.

They could hear the Tilden players yelling down the hall, a sound that got louder as they got closer to kickoff.

"They were making so much noise, we thought we were gonna die," Paul Barchitta said.

By the time Somma sent them out the door, reminding them that they weren't just representing their school and their families anymore, they were representing all of Staten Island, it might not have mattered what he said.

"It was like we were gonna have to kill them," Barchitta said, "before they killed us."

Right away, the first time he collided with the guy across from him, Billy Chambers felt the other kid buckle in a way he hadn't expected, and any anxiety he'd felt in the locker room drained out of him. These guys are big, he thought to himself, but they don't know how to hit.

There was still plenty of heavy lifting to be done, and they'd all have the bruises to show for it. But for the New Dorp kids, the championship game was going to be the final validation, if they needed any, of Somma's theorem that the hard way really was the easy way.

The first time Bliey got the ball, Romanolo hit him so hard he fumbled.

And that set the tone for the rest of the day.

When Bliey ran inside, Romanolo was there.

When he tried to bounce outside, Charlie Langere, all 148 pounds of him, was waiting for him.

The two Charlies, Romanolo and Langere, had been preparing for this day their whole lives. They just didn't know it.

They were tough kids. The kind of kids, Barchitta said, "who didn't take shit from nobody."

After high school, they both wound up becoming cops, put in their 20 years, then went very separate ways. After putting in his papers, Romanolo lived in San Diego and Las Vegas before settling in Windham, N.Y., in the Catskills, three hours north of New York City. He rarely went back to the Island, not even for New Dorp reunions.

"I don't know why," he was saying at his kitchen table in ski country.

He started to tick off the names ... Avena ... Esposito ... Boylan.

"I love those guys," he said.

Langere stayed home, became a community activist and a tireless advocate for kids, the kind who championed the cause of special-needs kids in the local Little League even when it meant taking on Little League headquarters in Williamsport. But like Barchitta, he was late coming to high school football.

"It was Sal Somma," he said, as if that explained everything, and maybe it did. "Somma and Milza, and New Dorp football. "They drew you in."

Romanolo got an earlier start. Like his next-door neighbor, Joe Avena, Romanolo had been playing all the American games for as long as he could remember, going from baseball to football to basketball, according to the season. In the summer, when they were just kids, Jeff Braman's father would stuff five or six of them into his two-door Studebaker, put a few more in the trunk, and drive them to Clove Lakes Park to play ball. The rest of the time, they had the PS 41 playground right across the street.

"Everything just kind of fit," Romanolo said. "It was a lifestyle. You came home from school, threw your books in the door and yelled, 'Mom, I'm going across the street!' Not that you had to tell her. She knew where you'd be.

"All you cared about was the next pitch, the next play, the next game."

In that "*Leave it to Beaver*," dinner's-at-6 world, where dads went to work and moms stayed home to take care of the kids, the toughest guys in the neighborhood looked forward to going to school. "I hear kids say they don't want to go to school," Romanolo said. "We never missed a day of school because if you didn't go to school, you couldn't go to practice.

"I don't know if Sal was really a disciplinarian, because he didn't have to be a strict disciplinarian.

"You respected him too much to do something stupid."

Baseball was Romanolo's game. By the time he got to high school, he was playing five or six games a week in the summer.

The night of the prom, he got home at 6 in the morning, and caught both ends of a doubleheader that afternoon. And after four years of butting heads with Fred Fugazzi and Marty Ryan every Tuesday, Wednesday and Thursday during football season, the only time he got hurt, other than some bumps and bruises, was the day he called for a fastball and Ronnie Isler, one of Somma's star tailbacks who wound up playing baseball at the University of Iowa, threw a curve.

At the last instant, Romanolo picked up the spin on the ball and whipped his glove hand across his body so hard the mitt flew off into the dirt, and he caught the ball bare-handed.

When he looked down, his thumb was bent at an angle he'd never seen before.

"Coach," he said, turning to the bench, "I think something's wrong."

But even for a baseball player, football season at New Dorp felt different. Somma was always warning them against believing their newspaper clippings, or acquiring a sense of entitlement.

"When the season's over," he'd tell them, "you're just another Joe." But the kids knew better. There was nothing better … after the Centrals manhandled Curtis in another Thanksgiving Day walkover … than walking into a basketball game in the Curtis gym wearing a New Dorp letter jacket.

"If you were a New Dorp football player, you were accepted everyplace you went," Romanolo said. "It was like, 'Hey, that's Billy Chambers!'

"When you're just a kid, who doesn't love that?"

Romanolo was the "other" back in the New Dorp offense, filling in for Fugazzi, Ryan or Truscelli, which meant he had to learn every position except wingback. And in Somma's regimented world, there was plenty to learn.

"Everything had to be just so," Romanolo said. Almost 50

years after he caught his last snap from Joe Avena, he jumped up from his kitchen table and got into a stance, demonstrating the blocking back's steps ... "one, two, three ... pitch" ... in the Single Wing "buck" series.

"If you did it wrong, he didn't chastise you ... he corrected you," Romanolo said. "But you never really claimed a position. Everybody learned to play different positions, and he moved guys around, especially on defense.

"Somehow he always seemed to get guys in the right place at the right time."

Marty Glickman, the play-by-play man on ABC-TV's *"High School Game of the Week,"* came to the job with a voice familiar to generations of New Yorkers after years of doing Knick games on the radio, and a repertoire of signature phrases that made his listeners feel like insiders. When Carl Braun or Willie Naulls made a jump shot and Glickman enthused, "Good ... like Nedicks!" everybody knew it was an homage to the orange drink and hot-dog stand outside the old Madison Square Garden.

Glickman, a fine football player and sprinter in his undergraduate days at Syracuse, had bitter memories of Downing Stadium, where he felt he got a bum decision in a photo-finish of the 100-yard dash at the same U.S. Olympic Trials where Jesse Owens emerged as a transcendent figure, and of the Games themselves. In Berlin, he and fellow sprinter Sam Stoller were replaced on the U.S. gold-medal relay team, presumably because American officials didn't want to irritate Adolph Hitler by having two Jewish athletes win gold medals.

But above all else, Glickman was a professional, and he took pride in giving the high school kids their due, and in getting all the unfamiliar names just right.

He called Romanolo and Langere's names a lot that afternoon.

The New Dorp kids felt like they were playing with a

stacked deck. Bliey was tipping the plays, leaning forward in his stance whenever he was going to get the ball, which was most of the time. But there was a price to be paid for all those head-on collisions with a guy who outweighed some of the New Dorp defenders by 80 pounds. Romanolo's ribs ached from all the times he threw himself in Bliey's path.

"He was a big guy," Romanolo said. "It was hard to wrap him up, so I just threw my body at his legs, and tried to cut his feet out from under him."

"I was like a welcome mat for him," Langere said.

Little Dennis Tancredi, who was listed on the New Dorp roster at 125 pounds and weighed less than that, had to be helped off the field, wobbly, after a ferocious collision with the next Jim Brown. A few plays later, he was back.

"We didn't know any better," Langere said.

He laughed, pointed at his head.

"Shit for brains," he said. But it was more than that. Like all good teams, the New Dorp kids had long ago graduated from hoping what Somma taught them would translate from practice to the games ... "What d'ya know, this stuff works!" ... to believing. That wasn't going to change because the other team made a lot of noise before the game, or the stud running back was bigger and faster than the guys trying to tackle him, and came preceded by his press clippings.

In a few short months, most of them — the captain and the streetfighter, the daydreamers and the tough guys — would be out of high school, and on their way to the rest of their lives. But that Saturday afternoon on the cusp of the turbulent Sixties, they were the perfect embodiment of Somma's Single Wing ethos ... eleven players, one agenda ... and sacrificing their bodies at the feet of the next Jim Brown seemed as natural as going down the Lane to Marty's for ice cream.

"I don't think I made a tackle all day," Marty Ryan said.

"Those little guys kept flying up there and hitting Bliey before he could get started.

"He never had a chance."

Bliey got his yards in the championship game. But they didn't come easily, or in big chunks. And Romanolo's pre-game assessment was on the money; with their big back held in check, Tilden didn't have a back-up plan. Bruce Rubin, the Blue Devil quarterback, completed all seven of his passes, but four of them went to the guys in the white shirts. Danny Boylan caught three of them. And on the other side of the ball, the Tilden defenders still haven't figured out the Single Wing.

Fugazzi, who ran for 150 yards and scored three touchdowns, was the best runner on the premises. When Tancredi caught a tipped pass just before halftime and kept right on going, all the way through the end zone and into the tunnel, the way Tom Hanks would do it in *"Forrest Gump"* a few years later, the Centrals led 30-0.

By the time Bliey got into the end zone in the final quarter, with Charlie Langere draped around his ankles, Somma was clearing his bench.

Whatever play Ryan called, the Centrals made it work. When Romanolo and Tancredi reprised the Statue of Liberty play from the previous week, and Pete Chiapperini leveled the last Tilden defender, they were only adding style points to a 42-6 walkover; one of those rare days in sports when the best team was at its best when it mattered most.

Almost 500,000 people within reach of ABC's television signal, broadcast from atop the Empire State Building, heard Marty Glickman declare Sal Somma's New Dorp Centrals the first official champions of New York City high school football; none any prouder than Carmine Avena, who couldn't wait until Sunday dinner to tell everybody he knew.

The shoeshine man from Quaglietta might not have understood the fascination Americans had with this strange game, played in fits and starts with a pointy ball that took funny bounces; but he knew that for one afternoon, anyway, his son was a television star, just like his favorite wrestler, Antonino Rocca.

An hour south of the city, Princeton coach Dick Colman, the Tigers' head coach after 20 years as an assistant under Somma's old pen pal, Charlie Caldwell, ducked into an office at halftime of Princeton's season finale against Dartmouth, just in time to watch on a snowy black-and-white television screen as New Dorp went in for another score.

"Hey, those are our plays," somebody said, recognizing the Single Wing action that was right out of Caldwell's book. But on that November afternoon when Somma's kids were scoring from everywhere on the field, and holding the next Jim Brown in check, it was hard to imagine anybody running it better than New Dorp.

"I think we could've beat the Giants that day," Bill Chambers said.

Back on the Island, they made a racket going down the Lane, and there was a crowd waiting for them at the high school. The victory party at Beth Crowe's house that night felt more like a coronation, and maybe it was.

But the Centrals had one more game to play.

18
Nothing to Lose

It was dark by the time the Curtis High School players finished practice the day before Thanksgiving. They finished the way they always finished practice, by running wind sprints and jogging laps around the field, because Andy Barberi never got to the part of the coach's manual that talked about going into a game with fresh legs. He was still running his guys into shape the day before the Thanksgiving Day game, the last game of the season, and the last game of organized football most of them … the seniors, anyway … would ever play.

Even in midlife, Barberi was still an unfiltered, untamed force of nature, the way he was that day at Yankee Stadium in 1936 when he kicked the stuffing out of Lombardi and the rest of the Seven Blocks: all menacing bulk and big hands, which he didn't mind laying on a wise guy if he'd already broken his quota of clipboards that day, with a voice like a riled grizzly.

"Hey, nipplehead!"

"Andy had his ways," Larry Anderson said. "But one thing you didn't do was challenge him."

Anderson, the honor student, student-body president, and three-sport star who called the plays when the Warriors had the football, knew all about that last part.

Barberi, as insecure as he was stubborn, was leary of asking for help, which meant he often coached alone. When he put in a new play at practice, that meant going over assignments one player at a time, while everybody else stood around and watched.

Early in the year, Anderson couldn't help wondering if the process might go smoother if they broke into groups and let somebody else — Jack Hurley, who was coaching Curtis' first-ever jayvee team, or Chester Sellitto, the Social Studies teacher who had been a star back at Wagner College, and was always offering to help — take the backs, while Barberi worked with the linemen. Or vice-versa.

His mistake was wondering out loud.

"What the fuck do you know about it?" Barberi exploded, chasing him off the field. "Get out of here! Go on, get the fuck out of here!"

Anderson was slumped in the locker room with his head in his hands, wondering if his high school football career was over because he'd spoken out of turn, when Barberi came to get him.

"What the fuck are you doing down here ... get back out on that field," he fussed, which was as close to an apology as anybody was likely to get from Andy Barberi.

Years later, when Anderson went back to teach and coach basketball at Curtis, Barberi was one of his staunchest allies, generous with his friendship and advice. But for the rest of the 1959 season, they barely spoke.

Most Curtis students got their introduction to Barberi on

their first day of school, when they were lined up on the gym floor and he hauled his five-by-five form onto a wooden platform above the bleachers and welcomed them, in his own politically-incorrect way, to high school.

"You're not suckin' your mommy's titties now," he'd tell them, before reminding them that they were on his turf, and God help the nipplehead who crossed him. "And don't let me catch you throwing any cigarette butts in the pisseria," he might add, inventing his own language as he went along.

"I don't come to your house and pee in the ash trays."

It was a different world, a world of flat-tops and bobby sox and parents who hadn't gotten around to worrying about how much playing time Junior was getting on the school team, or lawyering-up every time somebody uttered a disagreeable word in their child's direction.

In that world, a coach's word was law. Most schools had a guy like Barberi, or wished they had one, who kept the trains running on time from behind the scenes, and let the principal go on thinking he was in charge. Jim Regan, who went on to become President of the Board of Education, started his career as a substitute teacher at Curtis. "I thought Andy did everything," Regan said. "I didn't know the school had a principal."

When he was agitated, Barberi talked with his hands. And if he smacked somebody in the head to get their attention, or to drive home his point, he did it knowing that if some little wise-ass went home and complained to his father, he was likely to get a double dose of what Barberi gave him, just for getting the coach upset.

Dino Mangiero was 16 years old, already six feet tall and 230 pounds and a big high school football star the first time he got caught stealing, which was also the last time. He didn't have any money, and he picked up a candy bar in the school cafeteria and stuck it inside a book, and when the woman working the cash register saw it, he bolted.

Days went by. Mangiero avoided the cafeteria, and nobody came looking for him. He'd forgotten all about it when he saw Barberi coming toward him in the hallway between classes.

"Hi, coach," Mangiero said, "how ya doin'?"

Barberi hit him once, in the chest, and knocked him flat on his back. He was still stunned, trying to get his bearings, when he became aware of the coach's reddening face, alarmingly close, leaning over him.

"If I ever hear about you stealing anything again," Barberi said, "I'll kill ya."

The 60-minute hero of the Battle of the Bronx wasn't much of a coach. In the 13 seasons he'd been at Curtis, his football teams had lost more than they won, a record of mediocrity that looked worse than it was because the Curtis baseball and basketball teams, drawing from the same pool of athletes, were almost always the class of the neighborhood; and because he could never beat Somma in the game that mattered most.

While Somma huddled with Princeton's Charlie Caldwell, always fine-tuning the Single Wing, and spent hours choreographing each step ... Barberi's approach was reminiscent of Caldwell's college coach, Bill Roper, who believed the game was a battle of wills. *The team that won't be beat can't be beat.*

The Warriors ran the same offense and played the same defense every week, regardless of what the other team was doing. And if anybody was bold enough to complain that he was getting trapped or double-teamed, or he didn't know where the blocks were coming from, Barberi's answer was almost always a variation on the theme of "Get lower, hit harder," a message he commonly delivered with a healthy dose of four-letter words, and a smack on the head for emphasis.

Early on, his players learned to keep their helmets on when they went to the sideline.

More than once, Bert Levinson, the Curtis baseball and basketball coach, sat in the stands with him, watching a team the Warriors would be playing later in the season.

"What d'ya think," he'd ask Barberi.

"We're gonna kick the crap out of 'em," the conqueror of the Seven Blocks would say, as blind to the other guys' strengths as he was to his own team's shortcomings.

A few weeks later, if Levinson missed the game against the team they'd scouted, Barberi would call with an after-action report.

"We kicked the shit out of 'em."

"Hey, that's great. What was the score?"

"Aw, they got lucky ... we got beat 28-6. But we were knocking the piss out of 'em."

From where he stood, the other guys got lucky a lot.

The only people who saw another side of him were the ones who needed it.

If a kid got in trouble, after the yelling and smacking were over, Barberi would do whatever it took to help. He'd take the kid by the arm and go talk to the precinct sergeant, the district attorney, the lawyer or the priest. If Andy Barberi told them the kid wouldn't be any more trouble, that was usually good enough for them. The same kids he broke clipboards on were the ones he took to buy new shoes, because he knew things were tough at home. He was always going into his own pocket.

"He was crude and he was hard," Levinson said. "But when you needed him, he was the softest man you ever knew."

Bob Rinelli, Larry Anderson's football teammate, was cutting classes and headed nowhere good until the day he made the mistake of skipping Barberi's gym class. The next time he showed up, Barberi pulled him into a corner of the locker room, cuffed him around enough to let Rinelli know he was serious, and told him his days as a slacker were over. "And from now on," he said, "you're going out for football, so I can keep an eye on you." For the next two seasons, Rinelli was a two-way starting lineman for the Warriors.

"He kind of straightened me out," Rinelli said.

"He was tough, but he cared."

But for every tough kid Barberi scared straight, there were two more like Gene Mosiello, who might've been better players if they weren't so cowed by their coach.

Mosiello was one of Andy's guys, handed off from the parish priest to the high school football coach when there was nobody else to look after him, and a Curtis captain as a senior. Years later, when he was a prosperous orthodontist, Mosiello worked tirelessly to sustain a scholarship program in the coach's name, sometimes funding it out of his own pocket. But in 1959 Mosiello was just another scared sophomore, so afraid of doing something wrong when Barberi was around that he couldn't do anything at all.

"I know he meant well," Mosiello said. "It just took me a long time to figure that out." And there was a lot of that going around with the guys who played for Barberi.

Dino Mangiero survived Barberi's tough love and went on to play at Rutgers, and after that as a noseguard with the Kansas City Chiefs. When he came home to take a job as the football coach at Poly Prep in Brooklyn, where he coached the sons of Wall Street giants and corporate CEOs, the first thing he did was hang a portrait of Barberi on the wall behind his desk.

Somehow, through all the winning and losing, and a coaches' strike that put them on opposite sides of a bitter argument, Somma and Barberi maintained a relationship. Sue Somma and Eleanor Barberi bowled together. To Sal's children, Andy's wife was "Aunt Eleanor."

They were partners when it came to building the Thanksgiving Day tradition that sustained the football programs at both schools and kept high school football alive on Staten Island, and each was quick to jump to the defense of the other if he was being criticized. Even ... at least on Somma's end ... behind closed doors.

Barberi knew about the "informal" August workouts at New Dorp that were a violation of PSAL rules; and Somma knew he knew. "Andy never blew the whistle on me," he'd say, as if he understood how hard it might've been for Barberi to hold his tongue when he was getting his butt kicked in front of the whole neighborhood every Thanksgiving. If Somma resented the way Barberi jumped into his old job at Curtis, he never let on; and if Barberi felt guilty about it, he never let it show.

One Thanksgiving, a Curtis player ran down the field on the kickoff and punched New Dorp's Bob Ryan, who retaliated, and both players were tossed from the game. But when there were murmurs that the whole thing might've been premeditated — that Curtis was happy to sacrifice a nondescript player to take Ryan off the field — Somma squelched them. "Andy Barberi," he said, "would never have been responsible for this."

And, somehow, the Curtis kids always thought they were going to beat New Dorp on Thanksgiving, and wipe away everything that had gone wrong that season.

They just never did.

Nine times in a row, from the time Somma came home from Vermont and let everybody know the high school team was replacing the sandlot New Dorp Queens as the varsity on that part of Staten Island, his kids were the ones celebrating at Thanksgiving dinner. Just the year before, the Warriors got on the bus thinking it was their year, and got waxed 36-6. But they were kids, so they were resilient. Once they were in the middle of it, each season took on a life of its own, and the pain of the previous year's disappointments grew fainter with each passing week. It was like childbirth; by the time another Thanksgiving came around, they'd forgotten how much 36-6 hurt, and figured this was the year they'd get even.

And right from the start, 1959 felt different.

From the time the Curtis seniors entered high school, Barberi had been wed to the T-formation, and to running the football, using the same plays that hadn't worked the week before, or the week before that.

"If you can't get two yards when you need it, you don't deserve to win," he'd say when the other guys had nine defenders bunched at the line of scrimmage.

And, so, a lot of the time they didn't.

But after losing the '59 season opener, a disheartening shutout, the Warriors had two weeks to get ready for their next game. Barberi took advantage of the extra time, scrapping the T and going back to the Single Wing, the offense he'd abandoned along with most coaches across the country; the same one Somma was still using, with a few wrinkles, to win championships down at New Dorp.

Going on the road to play DeWitt Clinton, the largest high school in New York City, could be an intimidating experience. Before the game, one Clinton unit sprinted onto the field, ran a practice play, and made room for the next unit, and the next ... each eleven a little bigger and more polished than the one before ... until they had 90 or 100 kids out there. If it was possible, the Governors were even more intimidating than usual in the fall of 1959 with massive Gary Gubner, already a world-ranked shot-putter, starting at tackle.

If Barberi's kids were impressed, it didn't show. After the kickoff, they came out in their old T-formation and ran dive right and dive left, with predictable results. On third down they shifted into the Single Wing, and while the Clinton kids were still trying to figure out what was happening, Jim Barone, the Curtis captain, went 45 yard around end for a touchdown.

The next time the Warriors got the ball, Anderson took a re-verse 60 yards for another score, and they were on their way to a 26-0 upset.

"They had no clue what we were doing," Anderson said. "Nobody ever thought Andy would do anything different than what we always did."

After a hiccup against John Adams, Curtis won its last three regular-season games. For the first time in years, the Warriors would go into the Thanksgiving Day game with a winning record, and feeling good about themselves.

"Every other year, we'd go down the rosters, comparing man-for-man," Anderson said. "We always had good athletes, and we'd think, 'Hey, we've got a chance.' And then we'd get crushed. But in '59 there was no comparison. Esposito ... Fugazzi ... Marty Ryan ... Ryan was bigger than any of our line-men, and he was playing in the backfield. They could run, they could throw ... plus, they were city champs.

"We figured we had nothing to lose."

The Curtis kids watched the city championship game on tel-evision, rooting for New Dorp because they were the Staten Is-land team, and because some of them knew the New Dorp players from baseball or basketball. Now, as they ran laps in the dark the night before the last game, the Warriors were as loose as Anderson could remember seeing them.

They were halfway around the cinder track, in front of the covered grandstand that evoked images of a small-town minor-league ballpark, when the clear baritone voice of Carvin Young rang out above the sound of their labored breathing, and the steady crunch-crunch-crunch of their cleats on the cinders.

"*Stand up and cheer ...*" Young began to sing, and by the time he got to the second line, a dozen voices had joined in, then two dozen. Young didn't have to look around to know they were all singing along.

"Stand up and cheer ... stand up and cheer for Curtis High School ..."

Seven miles to the south, the New Dorp kids were crowded into a makeshift classroom in the basement of the high school.

It had been a short work week for Somma and the Centrals, who were coming off the emotional high of the city championship game, and nursing the bruises left over from all those collisions with Ron Bliey. Any other year, the Thanksgiving Day game would've been the focal point of their season; no matter how many times in a row New Dorp had beaten Curtis, everything else was foreplay. But for the New Dorp kids, the days following the Tilden game were like one long victory lap.

They couldn't walk down the hallway, or the street, without somebody wanting to tell them how they'd watched the championship game on television, and how proud they were.

Already, there were plans under way for a victory dinner, featuring Marty Glickman and Giant receiver Kyle Rote as guest speakers. Somma was invited to the Dapper Dan Dinner in Cumberland, Maryland, where somebody remembered that he'd grown up just across the river in the railroad hamlet of Ridgeley, West Virginia, before the floods and a railroad strike helped drive the Sommas north to Staten Island. He'd share the dais with Art Rooney, owner of the Pittsburgh Steelers, and Johnny Unitas, who made it back-to-back triumphs in NFL championship games against the Giants .

One national magazine had the brass to call New Dorp the fourth-best high school team in the country, although nobody had any idea how they could measure something like that. If it wasn't Thanksgiving week, it would've been easy to forget they had another game to play.

Every football season was full of rituals, especially at New

Dorp; none more cherished than the night before the last game, when the seniors told their teammates what it all meant to them.

This one didn't have the raw emotion of the meeting 10 years earlier, when Mike Dicenza implored the Centrals to beat Curtis and give themselves a season they'd remember the rest of their lives, and Paul Milza saw tears in the eyes of some of the toughest kids in the neighborhood.

"It was kind of subdued," Joe Avena said. "I think most of us were just sad that it was going to be over."

They went around the room, each of the seniors saying a few words.

Charlie Langere thanked Milza.

When it was Artie Truscelli's turn, the little tailback didn't hold back.

"This was the greatest thing that ever happened to me," he told them.

"I enjoyed every minute of it, even the 10 minutes I was knocked out."

19

What Country Are We Living In?

The night before the game, Barberi and Bert Levinson went to inspect the field at Weissglass Stadium, where Curtis played its home games. Levinson drove, the way he drove wherever they went, because Barberi had never learned to drive a car.

They were a curious pair, the Jewish basketball coach and the politically incorrect football coach. Barberi was as fluent in ethnic and religious stereotypes as he was in profanity — that was part of the time and place he came from, too; a time when Joe DiMaggio's teammates, some of them Italian, referred to their star as "the dago" — and he never felt the need to edit himself for Levinson's benefit. Or anybody else's, either.

He wasn't the only one. In Harry O'Brien's gym classes, dodgeball games routinely pitted the "guineas" against the "Micks." And if one group outnumbered the other, the "smoked Irish" could even the sides.

Theirs was a mutually beneficial relationship. During football season, Levinson served as Barberi's general manger, handling paper work, working the gate at home games, and making sure the referees got paid. When basketball season rolled around, Barberi did the same for him. But their friendship ran deeper than that, all the way back to when Barberi was still playing for the Long Island Indians, one step down from the NFL, and coaching the linemen at McKee High School, the vocational school just down the block from Curtis, and Levinson was a sixth-grader.

He was standing outside a high school game at Thompson's Stadium when he felt a hand on his shoulder.

"C'mon kid," Barberi said, taking him by the arm. When they got to the front of the line, he nodded to the guy collecting tickets. "He's with me," Barberi said, and they walked through the gate together.

Like a lot of more famous coaches, Levinson was never a star, not even in high school. He cracked the starting lineup in basketball when one of the other starters flunked off the team. And it wasn't until he was playing on an Army baseball team at Fort Carson, Colorado, with a feisty little second baseman named Billy Martin, who'd already made a name for himself in the 1953 World Series, that he felt like he understood the game.

But he knew he wanted to play. He wanted to play so badly as a kid that on Saturdays, when his father didn't approve of playing games on the Sabbath, he put his baseball equipment in a bag and dropped it out his bedroom window. Then he'd walk downstairs in a suit and tie, like he was on his way to synagogue, pick up the bag, and be on his way to the nearest ballfield.

And once he got to high school, Levinson knew he wanted to be a coach, like Harry O'Brien, who'd been turning out championship baseball and basketball teams at Curtis for as long as anybody could remember.

O'Brien had a personality that filled whatever room he was

in, bending referees and other coaches to his will, as if they were an extension of his program. "Like a god among gods," Levinson said, remembering when O'Brien would make up ground rules in the middle of a baseball game, or conduct a coin flip to decide home-field advantage over the telephone, from his office, while the other coach was in Brooklyn or the Bronx, waiting helplessly on the other end of the line.

"Uh ... too bad, you lost," he'd tell the other guy. "I guess you'll have to come here and play."

And because he was Harry O'Brien, he got away with it.

When Levinson got back from the Army, O'Brien let him coach the jayvee basketball team, the first time the older man didn't coach both teams himself.

"The first day of basketball practice, there'd be 125 kids on the floor, waiting to try out," Levinson said. "You'd walk down the line and tell a kid, 'Get a haircut or don't come back.'

"Whatever you said, they did, because they wanted that Curtis uniform."

He was 25 when O'Brien took him to meet James Corbett, the high school principal.

"This is your new basketball coach," O'Brien told Corbett, and that was that.

A few years later, Levinson succeeded O'Brien as the Curtis baseball coach, too. He won a ton of games in both sports, sent a bunch of kids off to play in college, and a few to the major leagues. He was at Yankee Stadium on Opening Day in 1967 when one of his guys, Frank Fernandez, hit a home run against the Angels, and he watched another one, Terry Crowley, come off the bench and help win a game for Earl Weaver's Orioles in the 1979 World Series.

The talent on Levinson's baseball teams was so deep that one year Fernandez was the starting catcher and a skinny, bow-legged freshman named Sonny Ruberto was the back-up catcher, and both of them made it to the big leagues. But he never forgot that first meeting with Andy Barberi, when he was a sixthgrader standing outside the fence at Thompson's Stadium.

For as long as he coached, Levinson never walked into the gym on game night without picking a kid out of the crowd on the sidewalk, and walking him to the front of the line.

"He's with me," Levinson would tell the guy working the door, and they'd walk in together.

The temperature was dropping through the 30s when Levinson and Barberi got to Weissglass Stadium, where the biggest game in the neighborhood had been played every Thanksgiving since 1952. Levinson fished a flashlight out of the glove compartment, and they walked across the track and onto the field, where the ground was getting hard after the previous night's rain.

Then they went to meet Somma at Gabe Rispoli's house.

Barker Street in West Brighton was a mix of blue-collar families, black and white, working people who shared the same hopes and dreams; and, in the years after World War Two, the same fear of Bill Morris's dog.

Morris, the son of the entrepreneur who founded the Staten Island branch of the NAACP, joined the Army before the war, when the armed services were still segregated. He fought in the Normandy invasion, and at the Battle of the Bulge, where he adopted a shaggy dog he somehow managed to smuggle home on a troop ship.

Everybody liked Bill Morris, who was a considerate neighbor, and good with kids. They weren't nearly as fond of his dog, which apparently thought West Brighton was still at war, and terrorized the neighborhood whenever she got loose.

"Trixie's loose!" somebody would yell, and people would scatter and watch from behind closed doors until she was back in the house, and the all-clear was sounded.

Rispoli's house was easy to find. It was the only one on the block with piles of 2x10 boards stacked in the back yard.

Weissglass Stadium, a hodge-podge of wooden bleachers shoe-horned into an asymmetrical space between a polluted creek, a railroad right-of-way and Memoly Motors, the local Dodge dealership, was Rispoli's second crack at owning a ballpark of his own.

The first one, which he named Gabe's Stadium, was built on leased land just across the creek, with surplus lumber the Army was offering to anybody who'd haul it away. It wasn't until Rispoli's guys were loading it onto trucks that they found out the wood had been used for temporary horse barns and pens. It was covered with manure.

"We washed it," Rispoli said, "but it still stunk.

"It stunk for a good long while."

When his landlords sold the land out from under him, Rispoli moved down the street and across the creek, to the site of the former Braybrooks Oval. But the bleachers at his old place had gone up so fast, and so easily, they gave him the idea for a new business venture. He started running portable bleachers all over the neighborhood, renting them out for horse shows, golf tournaments and parades.

Twenty years before big-league owners got the same idea, he went to the folks at the Weissglass Gold Seal Dairy, and for $500 he changed the name of the ballpark .

Before television taught Americans that if they sat in front of the set long enough, they could see just about anything without leaving the comfort of their living rooms, a generation of Staten Islanders grew up going to Weissglass Stadium — "going to Weissglass," they called it, the stadium part being assumed — to watch ballgames, rodeos, wrestling, and the regular Saturday night stock car races.

And, once a year, for the only football game that mattered in the old neighborhood.

Sonja Heinie, the Olympic figure-skating champion, performed at Weissglass. So did Carmine Avena's favorite wrestler, Antonino Rocca, who noted that that nobody at Madison Square Garden treated the wrestlers to pizza, the way Rispoli did. Eddie Feigner, the windmill pitching star of the four-man softball team The King and his Court, struck out some of the Island's best ballplayers blindfolded, from behind his back, and between his legs at Weissglass. Whitey Ford pitched there, when he was in the Army at nearby Fort Monmouth. So did Satchel Paige. And Josh Gibson hit a home run that cleared the Quonset hut-style roof of the car dealership beyond the right-field fence, bouncing into traffic on Richmond Terrace.

Fifty years before George Steinbrenner put a minor-league baseball team on Staten Island and New York Mayor Rudy Giuliani built a spanking new ballpark next to the ferry to house it, Rispoli had a baseball team he called the Staten Island Yankees. Those Yankees were really two teams: the neighborhood guys who played in the local Sunday morning leagues, and the semi-pro team that went around the Northeast playing town teams, Negro League clubs, and other semi-pro outfits like themselves. Before the big money changed everything, a decent ballplayer could do better living at home, working a fulltime job and making $10 or $20 a game on the side, than he could in baseball's low minors. And a lot of them did.

It was the traveling team that landed Rispoli in jail.

They warned him there might be trouble in Baltimore if he had black players traveling with the team. It was only a few hours from New York, but in the 1940s, before Branch Rickey and Jackie Robinson conspired to break baseball's color line, and before the city got a big-league franchise of its own, Baltimore might as well have been the Old South.

The problem was Rispoli had three black players on his roster: the Jackson brothers, Davey and George, and Bee Bush.

And nobody was going to tell him who he could play.

The Yankees made the trip in two cars from Sam's Taxi; and if the hotel wouldn't rent to black players, that didn't appear to be an insurmountable problem. Rispoli took a suite for himself, ushered Bush and the Jacksons up the back stairs, and put them in the adjoining room.

The police came for him in the middle of the night, knocking loud enough to wake everybody.

"Gabe Rispoli?"

"Yeah."

"You're under arrest."

He spent the night in jail, until one of his ballplayers reached out to the local baseball promoters. When they bailed him out, Rispoli had one question:

"What country are we living in?"

The host club — even then, they were the Baltimore Orioles — had a day-night doubleheader hanging in the balance, and hundreds of tickets already sold. But when they offered to loan him replacements for the three black players who spent the rest of the night trying to sleep in the cars from Sam's Taxi after they were rousted from the hotel, Rispoli balked.

"These are my ballplayers," he told the promoters. "If you want a game, this is my team."

That afternoon, with Davey Jackson on the mound, the Staten Island Yankees beat the hometown Orioles 1-0.

By the 1950s, semi-pro baseball was dying a natural death, done in by the same forces — television, major-league expansion, and the exodus of black stars to the big leagues — that killed the Negro Leagues. But the portable bleacher business was just taking off.

In time, Rispoli would follow it all the way to Florida. The 1959 Thanksgiving Day game would be the last time Curtis and New Dorp played at Rispoli's makeshift ballpark; but only because the game outgrew him, not the other way around.

After they checked the weather, Barberi, Somma and Rispoli would decide how many seats they were likely to need. Rispoli would do the math — 50 cents a fanny, one fanny every two feet — on the back of a brown paper bag.

One year, when the high schools were suffering through a budget crunch, he told Barberi and Somma he wouldn't charge them.

"But you put in all those extra seats," Barberi said. "Your guys have to get paid."

"Don't worry about it," Rispoli told him. "Next time I do a job at one of those fancy country clubs, I'll put it on their bill."

A lot of nights, when Barberi and Levinson were driving back from a late game or dinner, Barberi would nod off in the passenger seat, and sleep the rest of the way home. Sometimes … especially if it was a long drive, and Levinson was tired of driving in silence … he'd tap the brakes just hard enough to jolt Barberi awake.

"What was that?"

Levinson would mumble something about a careless driver cutting him off.

"Where is he? Let's get him!" Barberi would say, ready to administer vigilante justice. Curiously, none of the perpetrators was ever apprehended.

But this wasn't one of those nights; Bill Morris' dog wasn't around to harass them, and Levinson delivered Barberi home without incident.

A few miles away, in the house across the street from Semler's Park, where Marty Ryan learned to play football with his older brothers, the captain was already in bed. As he lay there thinking about the game the next day … the last game he'd ever play with Vic Esposito or Fred Fugazzi or Joe Avena, guys he sensed would be his friends for the rest of his life, and theirs …

Ryan found himself thinking about the Curtis players, and wondering if they thought they had a chance.

Down in Rosebank, where they took a practical approach to such matters, the bookies had Curtis as an 18-point underdog. In his column in the *Advance*, Hal Squier tried to have it both ways, noting that a sampling of local "celebrities" figured New Dorp to win by five touchdowns, but he himself expected a much closer game.

Ryan let the question sit there for awhile.

"Nah," he told himself. "They must know we're gonna win." And he rolled over and went to sleep.

20
What You Did

It was still dark when Sal Somma left the house Thanksgiving morning, on his way to pick up Andy Barberi; and maybe that was one more thing that could only happen in a place like Staten Island, where their lives had been overlapping for 30 years, since Al Fabbri brought them together at the high school where one of them still worked, and the other got a second start on life.

Tickets for the Curtis-New Dorp game had been on sale for weeks; at Earl's Sports Shop in Stapleton and Muche's in West Brighton; at Nanette's in Tompkinsville and the Sugar Bowl in Sunnyside and Marty's down in New Dorp, where Somma's student couriers made their covert ice cream runs. But a sellout was a foregone conclusion.

Football had been part of Thanksgiving on the Island for as long as either of them could remember, going back to the Stapes and Giants, and Curtis-Augies. Right from the start, when Paul

Milza and his buddy Charlie Kemether got to the ballpark before the gates were open in 1939, and Somma was on the other sideline, the Curtis-New Dorp game drew a crowd.

Official attendance for the '56 game, when the Centrals fulfilled Somma's prophesy by driving for the winning score just before the clock ran out, was 8,061; estimates ranged as high as 10,000, the biggest crowd to see a sporting event on Staten Island since that other Thanksgiving in 1929, when 13-year-old Wellington Mara took the ferry to watch his father's Giants play the Stapes, and there were people standing all the way up the hillside behind the ballpark.

Before television created millions of sports fans who never left their couches, Staten Islanders with no connection to either school followed the Curtis-New Dorp game from Thompson's Stadium to Gabe's Stadium, and then to Weissglass Stadium. Fathers took their sons, and the sons took *their* sons.

"It's like it was understood," Larry Anderson said. "Nobody ever complained about having to hold Thanksgiving dinner. They just asked what time the game was, and scheduled everything around that.

"It was what you did."

But all around them, change was in the air, and not just from the cold snap that had blown through during the night, turning the rain-soaked ground to concrete. Spurred by the launch of Sputnik I two years earlier, the U.S. was locked in a race with the Soviet Union to put a man in space. Halfway around the globe, the first American military advisers were killed in a place called Vietnam. And down in Atlanta a Baptist minister, just back from a visit with Mahatma Ghandi, was talking about building a nonviolent movement to secure civil rights for people of color.

Closer to home, a scale model of the new bridge, the one that would change everything on Staten Island, was on display in the lobby of the Staten Island Savings Bank in Stapleton.

Just up the street, on the site once occupied by Thompson's Stadium, where Somma scored a touchdown against Augustinian Academy on Thanksgiving morning and the New York Giants beat the Stapes on the same field that afternoon, ground was being cleared for construction of the Stapleton Houses, the city's first high-rise housing complex incorporating external balcony entrances, a space-saving concept borrowed from the Chicago Housing Authority. The last decaying remains of the old ballpark were carted off in dump trucks.

On the other side of the Narrows, Ebbets Field, abandoned by the Dodgers when they fled to California, awaited a similar fate. When the Curtis baseball team played there in the city championship game the previous spring, some of the old names .... Hodges ... Robinson ... Furillo ... were still on the lockers.

Almost a year had passed since the first homes were bulldozed to make way for the coming Clove Lakes Expressway, linking the new bridge to the New Jersey spans on the other side of the Island. By the end of the football season, almost the entire right-of-way had been cleared, a 100-yard-wide swath across the Island that separated the busy North Shore from the more rural South Shore in a way that, until then, existed only in people's imaginations.

It rained through most of the night on Tuesday, and into Wednesday. That night temperatures fell through the 30s, and it was still below freezing when Somma and Barberi got to Weissglass Stadium, eerily quiet at that early hour.

Even in that lonely setting, they were a mismatched pair: Somma, tall and dapper in his trench coat, jacket and tie, and ever-present hat; and Barberi, who always managed to look rumpled, as if he'd borrowed somebody else's clothes he'd found lying around the house. To cover his girth, he had to buy extra-large, and his raincoat hung almost to the tops of the work boots he wore everywhere, even in gym class. "Andy Boots," some of the New Dorp players called him, in a way that didn't sound complimentary.

Their stay at the ballpark was brief. The field was frozen solid — not even Barberi's boots left footprints — but there wasn't anything they could do about that. They stopped for coffee at the St. George Clipper, a diner just up the street from the famous ferry, already eager to get past the awkward goodbyes, knowing that in a few hours one of them was going to ruin the other's day, and his year.

"Good luck, Andy," Somma said when he pulled up at the big school on the hill, sounding like he meant it.

"Yeah … you, too."

Then they were free to be themselves.

The last bus ride of the year was as quiet as the first. Somma was in the first seat behind the door, as usual, with Milza to his left. Behind them were the steadfast trainers, Tex Dawson and Tom O'Connor, the usual platoon of student managers, and 10-year-old Rick Somma, the coach's son, in his first stint as the team's "valuables boy."

It was a 20-minute ride from New Dorp to the ballpark. No time for any one-on-one counseling sessions; and no need, this time, for Somma to reassure Artie Truscelli that he'd do just fine, or remind Marty Ryan not to give the new kid the ball until he had time to settle his nerves.

Somma was right, the way he'd been right about so many other things, that Saturday night when he told Milza they had the makings of a good team. The captain and the streetfighter … the jugheads and the student-body president … they'd all come a long way, together, since then.

A cop stopped traffic on Richmond Terrace, where the line of cars stretched as far as he could see in both directions, and waved the New Dorp bus into the Memoly Motors parking lot, just behind the stadium. Gabe Rispoli had an understanding with the local precinct captain; Somma and Barberi weren't privy to the details, but there was never a shortage of cops working traffic detail at Weissglass. Not even on Thanksgiving morning.

When the New Dorp kids took the field for warm-ups, they pawed at the ground with their cleats, but it was like trying to get traction on a tile floor. They went through their pre-game ritual on tippy-toe, taking mincing steps, trying not to wind up on the hard, cold ground. Then they headed back to the grease-stained solitude of Memoly's garage ... the closest thing to a visitors' locker room at Weissglass, where the home team shared a tin-roofed shack with boxes of hot dog buns from the concession stand ... to wait.

And wait some more.

Just a few miles away, the Curtis kids were going through their pre-game warm-up at the high school. This was one of Barberi's psychological ploys, one he'd tried before with middling success; the Warriors would warm up and have their pre-game talk at the high school, then show up right at game time, and come off the bus ready to play.

"They're not gonna start without us," he said.

They were coming off the practice field when Bert Levinson showed up, just back from Weissglass Stadium, where the field was starting to thaw.

"By the time the game starts, you could be playing in a swamp," Levinson told Barberi, and a few minutes later they were passing around boxes of extra-long mud cleats.

"Those New Dorp guys are going to be slipping and sliding all over the place," Barberi told his guys.

"You're going to kick their asses!"

The Curtis players met in M-56, the classroom across the hall from Barberi's cramped office, where they'd mustered before a hundred practices and games; or two hundred. But for the seniors, this would be the last time. The coach walked to the front of the room, and started to tell them how much the New Dorp game meant to him.

"Just get this one," he pleaded, more emotional than any of them could remember seeing him.

And before long, he started to cry.

Who knew where it came from? Maybe Barberi was tired of losing to Somma, and tired of people wondering why Curtis, still the biggest school on the Island by far, and the one with the richest sports history — the Castle on the Hill — always seemed to have the best baseball and basketball teams in the neighborhood, while the football team, which drew from the same pool of athletes, could never win the only game that mattered.

Maybe he was tired of looking the other way while Somma bent the rules, supervising summer workouts and happily playing all those out-of-district kids who allegedly went to New Dorp to study Italian, so they could talk to their sweet old grandmothers from the Old Country. Who did they think they were kidding?

Maybe, too, he was tired of keeping it to himself; because where he came from, you didn't run to some suit from the Board of Ed for help. You settled your differences on the field, even if that meant getting your lunch handed to you every year.

That dumb guinea ... that's what Barberi called Somma in his dark moments, when he was feeling shortchanged, as in, "That dumb guinea doesn't know what he's doing!" ... how did he corner the market on luck?

Somehow, through no fault of his own that he could see, Barberi had been stuck in Somma's shadow for most of his grown-up life, and the unfairness gnawed at him.

He, Andy Barberi, was the one who was a high school All-American; he was the one who captained NYU as a senior, and played with the College All Stars against the New York Giants.

He got kids into college, never played a kid who was injured, always tried to put the kids first in his smack-upside-the-head, tough-love kind of way. But at the end of the day, Somma always seemed to be the one taking the bows, a job Barberi would cheerfully have volunteered for; even that day at Yankee Stadium when he made hash of the Seven Blocks for all 60 minutes, and the headlines the next morning were about Somma kicking the winning point.

Even when he beat Somma back from the war, and settled into the only job either one of them ever wanted — and wasn't it just like Somma to fall into a state championship in Vermont? — somehow Barberi wound up with the short end of the stick.

Maybe, for once, he just wanted to see his guys go home for Thanksgiving dinner feeling good about themselves. Maybe the tears were a motivational tool, one last way of upping the emotional ante in the final minutes before kickoff.

The Curtis kids didn't know how to react. They sat there, terrified and mesmerized and feeling oddly moved at the same time, like spectators at a car wreck, unable to look away while the hardest man any of them had ever known sniffled like a baby.

"*Holy shit,*" they thought to themselves, "Andy Barberi's *crying!*"

21
Mud Season

When he wasn't staring down Baltimore cops or bigoted desk clerks, Gabe Rispoli had spent most of the previous 15 years promoting one kind of ballgame or another, trying to put fannies in the seats.

Now, for the first time in his life, he wondered if there might be too *many* people in the ballpark.

Every foot of the wooden bleachers that ringed three sides of the field, enough for 7,500 football fans, was filled an hour before kickoff. The overflow spilled onto the field behind the end zones and on both sidelines, where Rispoli's workers strung ropes to keep spectators from over-running the benches. People were hanging over the fence at the north end of the ballpark, where the wall was full of painted advertisements for local businesses .... *"When you think of style ... think of Archie Jacobson"* ... and from the cables slung to keep runaway tires or car parts from flying into the paying customers on race nights.

Somehow, a few kids had managed to climb onto the roof of the concession stand.

When he looked beyond the crowd, Rispoli noticed there were people sitting on the railroad trestle behind the western-most grandstand, where the occasional freight train still crawled along the river to the U.S. Gypsum plant in New Brighton. Somebody, Rispoli thought to himself, could get hurt before the day was over.

And there was still no sign of the Curtis football team.

The big crowd basked in the same mid-morning sun that was turning the field to goo, and the rumors started to circulate. Maybe the Curtis bus broke down. Maybe the Warriors were tired of getting their butts kicked every year.

Maybe they weren't going to show up.

It was six minutes past the scheduled 10:30 kickoff when they came off the bus and through the gate in their maroon and white uniforms, feeling the goosebumps when they saw the crowd. And when the people saw them, the whole place seemed to erupt at once: the Curtis fans because they were cheering for their team, and everybody else because after all the waiting, now they were going to see a football game.

Then the ball was in the air, and even Gabe Rispoli turned his attention to the mayhem on the field.

Bert Levinson was right. As quickly as the field froze the night before, it melted once the sun got to it. Now it was Mud Season in Port Richmond. The ooze sucked at the players' feet. It caked on their hands, their arms, and their faces, got in their eyes and their ears and their hair. In some places it was ankle deep; when they ran, it came up over their high-top shoes. On the sideline Jill Watson, one of the Curtis cheerleaders, walked right out of one of her shoes, which was mired in the mud.

Right from the start, Vic Esposito felt out of synch, a step slow, and he struggled to make sense of it. Was it just the mud?

The emotional letdown from the city championship game five days earlier? The long wait in Memoly's garage, wondering if the other guys were going to show up? Had the long, hard season caught up to the Centrals? Or was it just those tough Curtis kids on the other side of the line of scrimmage who had nothing to lose, and were playing like they thought they could win?

Esposito wasn't the only one. Early in the game, Fugazzi came out of a spin move and saw an opening as wide as New Dorp Lane. But the timing of the play was off by just a hair; the pulling guard, bogged down in the mud, was slow clearing the hole. Fugazzi clipped the guard's heel and went down, face-first in the mud. When Ryan tried to throw Running Pass, the play that had paid big dividends for the Centrals all season long, the mud-caked ball slipped out of his hand and popped straight into the air. Ryan caught it himself, before being run down by a wave of Curtis defenders.

For once, the Warriors weren't bewildered by the Single Wing, after practicing against it every day for two months. There was never a question about whether they were tough enough; most of the Curtis kids came from the same blue-collar roots as the New Dorp kids. But now the guys up front — Vinny Baldassano, James Jenkins, Paul Danneman and Carvin Young; Rinelli and Joe Montalbano and the fireplug middle guard, Tony Vitadamo — weren't falling for every fake. The linebackers weren't being sucked out of position. They weren't going away easy.

Most years, with 10 days to prepare after the end of the regular season, Somma added some new wrinkle for the Curtis game. A year earlier, the Centrals started the game by running all their plays from left formation, just to give the Curtis defenders a different look. But with four days between the championship game and Thanksgiving, Somma and Milza didn't have time to make major changes, or feel the need to get cute.

With both teams unable or unwilling to throw the ball, and slow-developing plays reduced to super-slow-motion in the mud, the game deteriorated into a primitive ballet of field position … tough guys against tough guys … not much different from that afternoon at Yankee Stadium, 20 years earlier, when Barberi slugged it out with the Seven Blocks.

Paul Barchitta watched all of it from the sideline. When Somma saw him clowning around at practice on Monday after the Tilden game, he benched Barchitta for the last game of his high school career.

It was just like Somma that he felt bad about it afterward. But he'd made a decision, and they'd both have to suffer the consequences.

"He came over and said he was sorry," Barchitta said. "But it was the best thing he ever did for me. There was a message there: you can't always be a horse's ass, and go through life being a Good Time Charlie.

"That's a lesson I carried with me the rest of my life."

From a distance, with both teams covered in mud, their uniform numbers obscured and the yard lines obliterated, the game took on a surreal quality: anonymous forms slamming into each other, dragging themselves up out of the muck, doing it again.

"Hey, don't take this for granted," Billy Chambers was saying in the New Dorp huddle. "Let's get it going!"

But it wasn't as simple as flicking a switch. There were two determined teams on the field, and the Curtis kids weren't playing to the script. With the threat of the New Dorp passing game all but nonexistent, and the outside game bogged down in the mud, the Curtis defenders crowded the line of scrimmage, and one or two of them hit Fugazzi on every play, whether he had the ball or not.

By halftime, with the game still scoreless, both Fugazzi's ankles were badly sprained; he could barely walk back to Memoly's garage. His facemask was split, his face broken and bloodied. He wouldn't finish the game. The next day, when he joined Ryan and Esposito for a *New York Journal-American* All-City team photo, his face was still swollen, his cheekbones an ominous shade of purple.

While the Centrals went to shiver in their wet uniforms in the dank recesses of Memoly's garage, where cigar smoke wafted in from the parking lot, Bert Levinson finished making his rounds of the ticket booths. A few minutes later he made his way onto the field, carrying a large duffel bag. He walked to the Curtis sideline, found a relatively dry spot alongside the bench, and sat on the bag, which bulged with $15,000 in small bills, enough to keep the football programs at both schools solvent for another year.

A few of the New Dorp kids took advantage of the break to change to mud cleats. But by then they had more to worry about than the footing.

"By then," Milza said, "the other team had confidence."

Somma's guys didn't win a city championship by accident. With their best runner on the bench, and the passing game that kept opposing defenses on their heels a distant memory, the Centrals put together their best drive of the day, all the way to the Curtis 13-yard line, where Truscelli was tip-toeing down the sideline on his way to another first down when he was hit from behind, and the ball squirted loose. "I never saw it coming," he said.

Curtis' Jim Jasinki fell on the football, and the threat was over.

The Warriors had barely moved the ball on offense. But the longer the game remained scoreless, the more the Curtis kids were emboldened to think the day belonged to them.

They seemed to draw strength from every play that didn't go for a touchdown against them; each stop a small sign that this year wasn't going to be like all the others when they started the day with high hopes, and had their spirit crushed by Somma's Single Wing machine. And as the third quarter bled into the fourth, the city champions were the ones who showed signs of unraveling. A holding call. An offside penalty. When Curtis's James Jenkins caught Truscelli for a 10-yard loss, Vic Esposito dropped back into punt formation, deep in his own end of the field.

In the weeks before the last game, Barberi had shown his kids an old lineman's trick for getting to the kicker. Now Tony Vitadamo, the Warriors' excitable middle guard, was lobbying for a chance to try it.

"Let's get it!" he urged Bob Rinelli, even more animated than usual.

Instead of rushing the punter when the ball was snapped, Rinelli hugged the nearest New Dorp blocker, and tried to pull him to the side.

At the same instant, New Dorp's Pete Chiapperini saw movement to his right. Later in life, the ex-cop and U.S. Marine would call Sal Somma's football team the most cohesive unit he'd ever seen. "We were disciplined because we wanted to be disciplined," he said. But this one time, instead of slowly giving ground the way he'd been taught, Chiapperini broke ranks, and took a step to meet the threat from the outside, leaving a gap where he'd been.

Esposito, who learned his rocking-horse kicking motion from Joe Somma, the coach's brother and a New York City police detective, was never the quickest punter, even under optimal conditions. But when had it ever mattered?

The one time it did, Tony Vitadamo came straight up the gut, untouched, and blocked the kick.

Marty Ryan, who moved into the line on punting downs to take Esposito's place at tackle, heard the "thwack" of the ball being kicked, followed immediately by a second "thwack" that sounded a lot like the first.

"I knew what that meant," he said.

The football hit Vitadamo square. It ricocheted backward, all the way to the one-yard line, where all Esposito could do was fall on it.

They were at the closed end of the ballpark, where the crowd stood 10 or 12 deep, pressed up against the end line and the sideline, and there was so much noise that when Larry Anderson called the play in the huddle, the Curtis kids strained to hear.

On first down, as the New Dorp defenders got into their stances with their feet and their backsides in the end zone, Curtis lined up in the T-formation, and shifted into the Single Wing.

Vin Riccardella, the Curtis fullback, tried the middle of the New Dorp defense.

Nothing there.

Vic Esposito was the first to hit him, a yard deep in the backfield, and Riccardella barely made it back to the original line of scrimmage.

On the next play Jim Barone, the Curtis captain, took the direct snap and started to the outside, while Larry Anderson tried to get in position to cut off Marty Ryan, coming hard from the middle of the field.

It wasn't the best block Anderson ever threw for Barone.

But it was enough.

Ryan, his initial charge blunted, regained his forward momentum and ran parallel to the goal line, hoping to beat Barone to the corner.

The Warrior captain, forced to belly back to avoid a mud-covered defender on the ground, went into a forward lean as he neared the goal line.

They met where the goal line meets the sideline, but Barone was already falling forward, into the end zone.

For an instant, there was no signal from the officials, as if even the men in the striped shirts were immobilized by the stunning turn of events. Then referee Mickey Fisher raised his arms.

Touchdown.

Curtis 6, New Dorp 0; first blood in the game that mattered most.

If it felt like the ground was shifting beneath their feet, that's only because it was.

Not only had Barberi's teams never beaten Somma's in nine previous tries; but New Dorp's 1959 city champs hadn't been behind in a game all season.

The idea that they could lose to Curtis had never crossed their minds. And they'd come too far, and gone through too much together ... picking up rocks on that dusty practice field behind the school, butting heads three or four days a week with Vic Esposito and Fred Fugazzi, giving up their bodies to stop the next Jim Brown ... to come apart the first time somebody knocked them down, or they got their noses bloodied.

Already trailing by a touchdown, the Centrals stuffed Riccardella's try for a two-point conversion.

Then Ryan, who had taken Fugazzi's place at fullback and would wind up with more rushing yardage than the entire Curtis backfield, put the Centrals on his back.

It never occurred to him that they weren't going to score. He'd already decided what extra-point play they'd run to win the game, the way they always won in the end. While the crowd pressed closer to the sideline, and sometimes over it, the captain ran for a first down, then another, barging straight ahead through the mud, leaving trails of bruised Curtis defenders on their hands and knees in his wake.

Then Truscelli, still a mass of foam rubber and athletic tape after all the late-season injuries that had taken a toll on his body, followed a convoy of blockers around end for 20 yards through the mud, to the Curtis 14-yard line.

On first down, Ryan spun for three yards.

On second down, Truscelli lost three.

Still ten yards from a fresh set of downs, 14 yards from the touchdown that would change everything, with Fugazzi on the bench and Truscelli's spare frame not designed for battering against an eight and nine-man defensive front — a welterweight caught in a heavyweight fight, even if he was a willing welterweight — Ryan called his own number.

On third down, he got two yards.

On fourth down, he got two more.

The Curtis defense had held. The Warriors took the ball back on downs, their 6-0 lead looking bigger with each second that came off the clock.

All season long, Larry Anderson had been calling the plays for the Warriors without imput from Barberi, and he didn't need anybody to tell him how to handle the final minutes of the game of their lives.

"We're going to run the same play every time," he told them in the huddle. No handoffs, no mistakes, no penalties. Keep it simple. Let the clock be their friend.

"Thirty-eight smash," Anderson said.

Fullback off tackle.

Years later, Vin Riccardella would earn a reputation in the New York City fire department as the kind of guy who was at his best when you saved the toughest jobs for him, and let him know the whole thing was on his shoulders. The Curtis kids could've told them all about that.

"That's who he was," Anderson said.

Four, five, six times in a row, Anderson called Riccardella's number, and the big fullback banged straight ahead, getting three yards here, four there, a few more the next time .. just enough to eke out a first down, then another, and keep the clock moving.

When he couldn't think of anything else to do, Charlie Romanolo lay down in the mud, pretending to be hurt; anything to put off the unthinkable.

"We weren't supposed to lose," he said.

"It was impossible."

One of the officials walked over and told him to get up and play football.

In the Curtis huddle, there was no anxiety, only a kind of energy none of them could remember feeling.

"Thirty-eight smash," Anderson said.

And then, just before they went to the line, something else. "This is the game."

The Curtis team that broke the huddle wasn't the same one that opened the season by losing to Flushing, or the one that went 3-2 in the PSAL's Queens-Staten Island division; or even the one that started the day with nothing to lose, watching Andy Barberi cry.

Barone. Baldassano. Anderson. Riccardella. Rinelli. Vitadamo. Jenkins. Jasinski. Montalbano. Young. Danneman. Guy DeMauro. Al Carbone. Carl Ettlinger. Bob Corsale. Jim Warren. Ray Ferro.

Whatever happened in the next few moments, they were already part of a game that nobody who was at Weissglass Stadium that day would ever forget; the kind a guy takes with him, and holds close, no matter what else he does in his life.

Together, they settled into their stances.

"This is the game!"

22

No Second Chances

And then it was over.

Vinny Riccardella wrapped both hands around the football, leaned into the backs of Guy DeMauro and Bob Rinelli, and fell forward, one last time, into the mud; and in that instant the clock expired. Referee Mickey Fisher took the ball and held it over his head. Just like that, there was no more football left to be played. No do-overs, or second chances; no opportunity for the New Dorp kids to redeem themselves, to correct a terrible mistake, which is how it felt.

For them, the next few minutes were a haze, seen through the blur of their tears.

As soon as he got home that afternoon, Vic Esposito went straight to bed, and when he woke up he tried to convince himself it hadn't happened.

"My mind didn't want to accept it," he said.

Years later, most of them had trouble recalling the moments

immediately after the game, like trauma victims who can't remember anything after the accident.

There were no handshakes between winners and losers. No hugs, and no prayer circles like the ones that started appearing on television a few decades later, with players from both teams holding hands. A few years earlier, when he was a sophomore and his friend Bobby Campbell was the Curtis captain, Marty Ryan had run downfield under a punt and hollered, "Look out, Campbell!" just before he bowled him over, and it all seemed like great fun. Not now.

Thirty years later, Ryan would look backward from the second half of a life lived in full, and tell his high school teammates that he'd been on the losing side in four Army-Navy games ... including the one when he sat in the stands with his dislocated vertebrae, wondering if he could've made a difference ... and none of those defeats stayed with him like the day New Dorp lost to Curtis in the mud. But in the immediate aftermath there was only an overwhelming sensation of helplessness, as the New Dorp players fought to keep their emotions in check, to hold back the tears until they were away from the crowd, back in the anonymity of the team bus.

Not all of them made it.

Their tears carved tracks down their mud-caked cheeks, turning their faces into mourning masks, and they didn't have the strength to reach up and wipe them away.

A stranger took Danny Boylan by the arm and led him to where a photographer was trying to stage a picture with Jim Barone, the Curtis captain, who scored the game's only touchdown. Somebody had chosen Boylan and Barone as the game's outstanding players, which meant they'd be invited to the Downtown Athletic Club a few weeks later to see LSU's Billy Cannon get his Heisman Trophy.

One of the grown-ups leaned over to say something and Boy-

Ian smiled, more out of reflex, or politeness, than because it was anything he thought was funny.

Out of the corner of his eye, he spotted Somma, whose face looked like it might crack.

"Get that smile off your face," he said, in a tone that indicated he wasn't close to kidding.

Somma was fighting his own losing battle with his emotions. When Esposito came to him feeling guilty because it was his punt that was blocked, Somma claimed responsibility, saying the loss was his fault, that he should've done a better job of preparing them in the days between the city championship game and Thanksgiving. But in those gut-wrenching moments after the game there was nothing to do but go home, so he shepherded them onto the bus, where Andy Barberi suddenly appeared, wanting to console the losers.

Somma didn't want any part of it.

"I didn't go into your locker room the last nine years," he growled, and for once there was a hint of malice in his voice, the way you imagine there must have been that night in Rosebank when he went looking for the sandlot baseball coach who'd crossed a line, and the other guy wound up going through a plate glass window. In the back of the bus, the thought went through some of their minds that Somma might hit Barberi, and right at that moment there may have been a few of them wishing he would. But Barberi, full of himself the way only a man who'd waited so long for such an opportunity could be, didn't seem to notice, or else he didn't care.

He shrugged off Somma's objections, and climbed into the doorwell of the bus.

The New Dorp kids shouldn't feel so bad, he told them, pleading his case to an audience that couldn't hear, or wouldn't, the words sounding lame even as they left his mouth. Even in his exuberance, it must've registered somewhere in Barberi's mind that it wasn't working. He'd been waiting for a day like this his whole football life, since that afternoon at Yankee Stadium when he kicked the stuffing out of the Seven Blocks of Granite, and already it wasn't unfolding the way he'd imagined it would.

For a few long, awkward seconds he teetered there at the top of the bus steps, unsure whether to press on, or flee back down to the pavement where it had been easier to breathe.

"You're still champions," he managed to get out, almost defiantly, flinging the words toward the back of the bus, like the last volley in an argument he was losing to himself. Then he wobbled back down the steps and onto the pavement, everything but his hat already out of sight, even before the doors closed behind him.

And that was it. The season was over; and for the seniors, so was high school football. A bunch of the New Dorp kids would go on to play in college, but somehow they already sensed it wouldn't be the same.

Alone in the yellow school bus, their grief seemed compounded, as if they were crying not just for what had been lost ... the game, and the perfect season, and the game ball Marty Ryan would never see, because for the only time anybody could remember, Sal Somma got ahead of himself ... but for everything that was about to be lost: a way of life they wouldn't miss until long after it was gone, along with the place where they grew up, which would soon be replaced by a Staten Island they wouldn't recognize ... and an uncomplicated time in their lives when everything revolved around football, and each other. And like the game that had just ended, once that time was gone, it was gone forever, and there was no getting it back.

"Let's go," Somma said, and the bus lurched into gear, inching into the endless line of cars on Richmond Terrace, ferrying Staten Islanders home to Thanksgiving dinners where nobody would believe their stories until they saw the headline in the next day's *Advance*, right up there on the top of the front page of the newspaper, above the banner. Then they were around the corner, leaving Barberi standing in the parking lot, alone, in the hour of his triumph.

To 10-year-old Rick Somma, sitting a few rows behind his father, it felt like the whole order of things was coming apart. With the doors closed and the windows fogging over, they were in their own self-contained world, bouncing along potholed streets toward a future that felt less secure than it had a few hours ago, the terrible silence broken only by the sniffling going on around him. It was unnerving, seeing all those big guys, tough guys, bawling like babies.

Then he felt the tears stinging his cheeks, and realized he was crying, too.

Epilogue

The next season, the New Dorp football team limped into the Thanksgiving Day game with a middling 3-3 record, but there were no calls to avenge the '59 team, or the perfect season spoiled; at least not from Somma.

"That wasn't his style," Bob Ryan said.

The Centrals left nothing to chance, beating Curtis 16-0, the first of three straight Thanksgiving Day shutouts. Back to business-as-usual.

It would be eight years before Curtis won another Turkey Day game.

The rivalry lost some of its shine when the new Catholic school in the neighborhood started a football program. Before long, Staten Island had six high school teams. But when some of the other public-school coaches complained that they couldn't compete with Monsignor Farrell, a magnet for every Catholic kid on the Island who wanted to play football, Somma and Barberi refused to join the chorus, even though Barberi's teams never won a game against the new guys.

"Over my dead body," he'd say, just like he did when he and Somma had the only show in town, whenever anybody suggested sacrificing neighborhood rivalries like theirs in the name of an expanded playoff format.

It was no coincidence that six months after Barberi died, Farrell stopped playing the public schools, and Curtis was demoted to the public school league's B Division. For the first time in 28 years, New Dorp didn't play Curtis on Thanksgiving Day.

Officials at the two schools tried to revive the game a few years later, only to be reminded that it's not a tradition if you only do it some of the time.

By the turn of the century, Staten Island had 10 high schools playing football. But the public schools and Catholic schools continued to play in separate leagues, and the crowds for most of those games were a fraction of what the once were.

The Bridge — for Staten Islanders, the Verrazano-Narrows would quickly become "the Bridge," in the same way Manhattan was "the city" — exceeded the experts' most dramatic traffic projections. The lower deck, originally scheduled for a 1975 opening, was rushed into service in 1969. The toll George Scarpelli paid with a Kennedy half-dollar in 1964, when he drove the first car full of his friends across the new span, was up to $10 in 2008.

In the first 40 years of the bridge's life, the Island's population more than doubled, to almost half-a-million people. The usual émigrés from Brooklyn and the Bronx were joined by a new wave of immigrants from Russia, Africa, and Eastern Europe.

The lines between neighborhoods blurred as towns ran together, swollen by a flood of newcomers who identified more with Bensonhurst or East Harlem or Lagos, Nigeria, than this new place, and weren't interested in the high school game going on down the block. But the Island remained a blue-collar enclave, more provincial and more conservative than the city as a whole, and home to a disproportionate number of cops and firemen.

Seventy-eight of the 343 firemen who died at the World Trade Center on September 11, 2001 were Staten Islanders. St. Clare's, the little Catholic church where the New Dorp guys from '59 and those from '64 carried Sal Somma's casket past the columns of high school players in their football uniforms, lost eleven of them. Among the dead Staten Island firemen was Stephen Siller, whose sacrifice was symbolic of the uncommon courage that was the norm in the hours after the hijackers flew the planes into the buildings. Off duty and on his way to play golf with his brothers at the time of the attack, Siller drove his truck as far as the Brooklyn approach to the Brooklyn-Battery Tunnel, which was closed to everything but official vehicles. He parked the truck, threw 75 pounds of gear on his back, and started running through the tunnel, until a passing engine company stopped to pick him up, and delivered him to the towers in time to die.

Robert Moses, the driving force behind the construction of the Verrazano-Narrows Bridge, relinquished his position as chairman of the Triborough Bridge and Tunnel Authority amid growing criticism over massive urban renewal projects that showed little regard for the quality of life in the neighborhoods most directly affected. Even worse, in the eyes of some Dodger fans, Moses was partly responsible for the team's flight to California, having opposed Walter O'Malley's attempts to build a new ballpark in downtown Brooklyn.

Weissglass Stadium closed for good in 1972, after a rash of fires and vandalism. For the next 30 years, the site sat empty and largely unused, except as an occasional depot for out-of-use construction equipment, or rusting machinery sinking into the mud.

Gabe Rispoli, who continued to provide portable bleachers for the Curtis-New Dorp game when it was moved to Port Richmond High School, moved his headquarters to Florida, where there was more year-round work. His company, Florida Grandstand, handled the set-up for the annual Orange Bowl Parade, all the big golf and tennis tournaments, and nine Presidential inaugural parades.

Seven of New Dorp's 11 starters played college football. Vic Esposito played in the Gator Bowl. Marty Ryan played in the Army-Navy Game with President John F. Kennedy sitting in the stands. Joe Avena, Bill Chambers and Danny Boylan all followed Fugazzi to Missouri Valley. Only one of the Curtis seniors, Vin Riccardella, played in college ... at Wagner, the school one hill over from the high school.

And while the winners of the Thanksgiving Day game went their separate ways after high school, the losers seemed to grow closer with the passage of time, as if Somma was still pulling the strings; still getting them to want for themselves the same things he wanted for them.

A half-century later, from a condo in Boynton Beach, Fla., Pete Chiapperini reached back over the years to take responsibility for the blocked punt in the Curtis game.

"That game's on my shoulders," he said, remembering the one time he broke discipline, and opened a lane for Tony Vitadamo to get to the punter.

But by then it no longer mattered; and maybe it never did.

"I've thought a lot about that," Avena said. "A loss like that might've torn another team apart.

"We don't talk about it much. But in all the times we've been together, I've never heard anybody blame anybody else, or even question what happened.

"We had all those experiences together ... and it was like we shared that, too."

The first few winters after they graduated from college, Avena, Ryan, Esposito and Fugazzi rented a ski house together.

As a freshly minted Army second lieutenant, Ryan could buy beer at the PX for $2 under the civilian price. "We figured we saved about $5,000 the first winter," he said.

In the years that followed, they stood up for one another at weddings and christenings.

And sometimes at funerals.

After they got over the shock -- Fred Fugazzi died trying to *break up* a fight -- his friends organized an all-star game and a scholarship fund in Fugazzi's memory. Avena got the other Staten Island high school coaches involved. Artie Truscelli sang the national anthem. Together, the old Centrals kept the game and the scholarship going, so it became one more way they bonded.

At one of the first Fred Fugazzi Memorial Award dinners, a short, smiling man approached Vic Esposito's wife. "I'm the guy who blocked the punt," Tony Vitadamo said, and nobody had to ask which one he meant. A few years later, the surprise hero of the Thanksgiving Day game was dead, after contracting a tropical disease in South America, where he'd gone into business exporting exotic pets.

In an effort to connect younger players to the school's storied past, Somma and Avena helped start a New Dorp Football Hall of Fame. The induction ceremonies turned into raucous re-unions, filling the biggest banquet rooms on the Island, where emcee Tony Brandefine's threats from the dais -- "Don't make me come back there and beat you up!" -- were a cover for the undercurrent of love.

But not everything was done with a nod to the past.

The high school polled students to choose a new nickname for the school's athletic teams, one that would lend itself to having a costumed mascot. (Nobody could say for certain what a Central was supposed to look like.) "Cougars" got the most votes, and when the alumni raised a stink, they settled on the Central Cougars, which didn't satisfy anybody.

Even the Princeton-inspired striped jerseys were phased out when manufacturers and suppliers started charging custom prices.

Andy Barberi won his last game as a high school coach ... beating New Dorp by the slightly ironic score of 6-0 ... on Thanksgiving Day 1974.

When he died, his former players established a scholarship in his memory. A few, like Bill D'Ambrosio and Gene Mosiello, the tailback who believed Barberi scared him out of being the player he might've been, kept it going with their wits and their resolve; and sometimes, especially in Mosiello's case, with money out of his own pocket.

The football field at Curtis is named for Barberi; and Ralph Lamberti, an undersized Curtis fullback before he was the Staten Island Borough President, led a successful campaign to have a ferryboat named for him.

Sal Somma coached at New Dorp until he was 66. When his admirers conspired to have the field at the new high school named for him, it was the first time a Board of Education facility was named in honor of somebody who was alive to see it. And when the football coaches at McKee/Staten Island Tech resurrected the Single Wing, Somma came out of retirement in his 70s, and coached the McKee junior varsity to an undefeated season.

In the last years of his life, he edited a history of high school football on Staten Island, a book that wasn't nearly as much about him as it should've been, and campaigned for a War Memorial Stadium, the kind of place that could've held all the people who wanted to see Curtis play New Dorp when there were only two high school teams on the Island, and one game that mattered more than all the others.

The idea for a Staten Island Sports Hall of Fame came out of the basement of Sal and Sue Somma's ranch house, which had become the repository for so much of the history he witnessed, or helped make. Kids shouldn't have to go all the way to Cooperstown, he reasoned, to learn about what Bobby Thomson did that afternoon in 1951, when he hit the home run that broke Brooklyn's heart.

Right from the start, Somma's name was like a passkey for the Hall of Fame committee, opening doors at the Borough President's office, and at the College of Staten Island; the difference between getting something done and wishful thinking.

He missed the inaugural induction ceremony by two years.

When one of his former players happened upon him in the hospital and wondered why he hadn't let anybody know he was sick, the response he got was heartbreakingly Somma-esque.

"I didn't want to bother anybody," he said.

When the Hall of Fame got around to inducting its first class, it was a big deal in the old neighborhood. The ceremony was held at the College of Staten Island's Williamson Theater, a venue built to celebrate Mozart and Shakespeare. The committee members showed up in tuxedos, and the inductees wore boutonnieres and corsages. Bobby Thomson was part of the first class, one more testimonial for the man who hit the most famous home run of them all, and took the ferry home from work; so was Mike Siani, who played for Somma at New Dorp and went to a Super Bowl with the Oakland Raiders.

But when it was time to call the roll, a few days after another Thanksgiving without a high school football game on Staten Island, Somma's name was the first one called, ahead of Thomson and Siani and a roster of big-leaguers, Olympians, and All-Americans.

All these years later, he remains the only honoree introduced out of alphabetic order.

Joe Avena wasn't the only one grateful for that uncomplicated time when football was all they had had and all that mattered, and the last thing some of them did for love, and Somma gave them a reason to believe in themselves, and each other, and permission to dream big.

"I like to think Sal Somma's example got me through life, despite my character flaws," Paul Barchitta was saying at the end of a career as a teacher, coach, and athletic administrator. "You wanted to be him, even though you knew you didn't have his personality."

That part hadn't changed since the first time any of them sat in a locker room, listening to Somma appeal to their pride in the anxious moments before kickoff, hoping they wouldn't do anything to disappoint *him*.

"If it wasn't for football," Barchitta said, "I don't know if I would've survived."

Fifty years after the New Dorp kids left Weissglass Stadium with tears carving streams through the mud on their faces, Vic Esposito and his wife celebrated New Year's Eve with the Avenas.

The next day, they had dinner with Danny Boylan and his family.

A few months later, back in his office in Virginia Beach, Esposito was recalling their most recent conversation on the phone.

"One more thing I gotta tell you before we hang up," Boylan told him.

"I love you."

Esposito's whole life had been informed by the years he spent playing football for Sal Somma at the red brick school where he found a guidebook for living, the way Avena found a calling, and Dan Boylan's son found himself.

When they were still boys, Esposito lived through a dream season with these men, and watched it snatched away in a manner that only served to draw them closer. Now he felt rich in ways money could never buy, with friends he could call at any hour of the day or night and ask for help, and know they'd be there for him, the way he'd be there for them, these men he wasn't embarrassed to say he loved.

Along with everything else, when they hadn't known it was happening, Somma had given them each other.

A half-century after they lost the last game in the mud, that might've been the greatest gift of all.

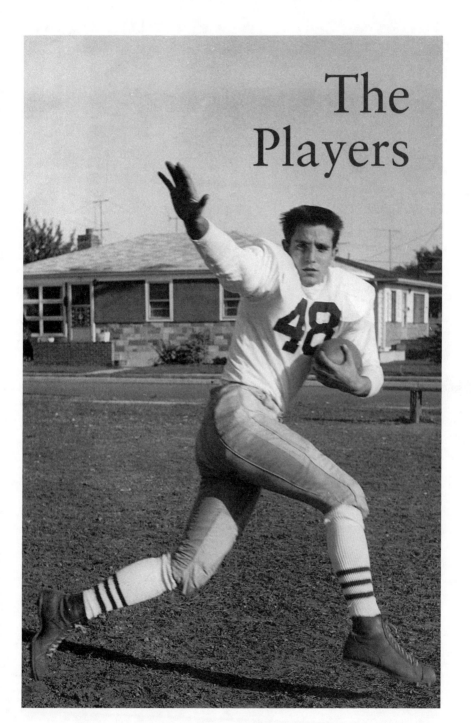

The
Players

Thanksgiving Day

1959 Curtis Warriors

No.		Pos	Ht.	Wt.
3	Destafano, Daniel	E	5-10	165
4	Rymas, John	T	6-0	190
5	Jasinski, James	C	6-0	175
7	Carbone, Al	G	5-8	175
8	Baldassano, Vincent	HB	5-10	155
10	Danneman, Paul	E	5-8	175
12	Ferro, Ramon	QB	5-8	150
13	Davis, Ron	B	5-9	145
14	Anderson, Larry	HB	5-9	165
15	Warren, James	B	5-9	165
16	Moramoraco, Ventura	G	5-5	170
17	Maniscalso, Charles	HB	5-8	165
18	DeMauro, Gaetano	T	5-8	175
19	Young, Carvin	E	6-0	170
20	Corsale, Robert	FB	6-0	175
22	Lenza, Anthony	QB	5-6	140
23	DeFazio, Victor	T	5-9	195
24	Johnson, Charles	T	5-10	215
25	Ettlinger, Carl	QB	6-0	165
26	Riccardella, Vincent	FB	6-0	190
27	Barone, James	HB	5-7	155
30	Jenkins, Ray	T	6-0	190
31	Montalbano, Joseph	T	5-10	195
32	Monasseri, Ben	G	5-9	165
33	Gatto, Vincent	G	5-6	165
34	Vitadamo, Anthony	G	5-8	165
35	Rinelli, Robert	G	5-10	190

November 26, 1959

1959 New Dorp Centrals

No.		Pos.	Ht.	Wt.
1	Ryan, Marty	B	6-1	195
3	Langere, Charles	B	5-9	148
4	Tancredi, Dennis	B	5-7	125
5	Springer, Lou	B	5-10	160
6	Parello, Tom	B	5-7	128
8	Keller, Larry	G	5-2	150
9	Shotwell, Henry	T	5-9	157
12	Curran, Jerry	T	6-0	165
13	Liozzi, Bruce	G	5-6	160
14	Cole, Ken	E	6-1	165
16	Johnston, Doug	B	5-9	141
22	Johnson, Bob	T	6-3	180
23	Panzica, Rich	T	5-5	175
25	Rathke, Fred	G	6-3	180
26	Samulski, John	E	6-5	190
27	Twiste, Bob	C	6-0	185
29	Pecoraro, Dennis	C	5-10	180
32	Jones, Walter	B	5-11	140
33	Truscelli, Art	B	5-5	135
35	Boylan, Dan	E	6-2	170
36	Barchitta, Paul	E	6-1	170
37	Mazzella, Anthony	B	5-4	134
39	Romanolo, Charles	B	5-9	170
41	Peace, Don	B	5-9	155
42	Chambers, Bill	E	6-2	176
43	Tait, John	T	6-2	180
44	Cavallo, Matt	G	6-0	175
45	Avena, Joe	C	5-10	172
46	Miceli, Lou	E	5-10	180
47	Baggs, Wm.	B	5-7	145
48	Fugazzi, Fred	B	6-0	176
50	O'Prey, Mike	T	6-0	162
51	Thompson, Dennis	T	5-11	175
52	Esposito, Vic	T	6 1	195
53	Chiapperini, Pete	G	5-9	195
59	Russo, Lou	G	5-10	175

Acknowledgements

It all starts with Sal Somma, the way so many of the good things in the old neighborhood start with him.

It ends here, because of people like Joe Avena, who must've been tired of hearing me say I was going to put it all in a book; and all the others who told me their stories over the years:

Rick and Toni Somma. Marty, Joe, and Bob Ryan; Vic Esposito, Artie Truscelli, Danny Boylan, Paul Barchitta, Charlie Romanolo, Bill Chambers, Charlie Langere and Pete Chiaperrini. Bert Levinson, Larry Anderson and Bob Rinelli. Tony Brandefine. Funzy Chioffi and Roy Rotella in Vermont. Larry Ambrosino, John Iasparro, Bob Sambataro, Joe Tetley, Jay O'Donovan, Bruce Liozzi and the backfield firm of Mickey Burns and Jim Fagan. John Pecoraro, Lou Formica, Joe Clark and Ben Sarullo. Gene Mosiello and Dino Mangiero. Hall of Famer Ken Strong. Mary Koffer and her daughter Betty, who took me into their home, and sat me at the kitchen table where Al Fabbri convinced Anthony Somma to let Sal quit his job at the B&O rail yard to start a new life. One of my big regrets, Mary, is that I won't get to read this to you.

Paul Milza, who deserves every ounce of the respect and gratitude his former players show him.

And Wellington Mara, a gentleman right to the end.

None of it happens without Charlie Perrino, the go-to guy for all things New Dorp. Monsignor Ed Whelan. Russ Siller and Paul Macko. Kevin Flood, Charlie Greinsky, and Jack Tracy. Tracy's college roomie, John Monteleone, who still has the passion that made him such a good ballplayer.

Tom Quinlan, who treated me the way he treats a lot of people: as if we'd done something to deserve it.

Laura Gringer, one of the more patient people on the planet.

Tom Doherty.

And Cormac Gordon, who talked to me like the friend he is.

Closer to home, Boomer, Bryan and Sean, my favorite football players, who wouldn't let me pack it in.

Renée, Laura, Evan, and Darryl, who made me feel like part of the family; and Christopher, who took a bunch of words and made them look like a book, nothing less than that. And Nancy, my ideal reader, who held my hand every step of the way, and lived this story with me.

Book design by Christopher Johnson